Whales
Dolphins and
Porpoises

Written and photographed by
Mark Carwardine

For Mum and Dad – thank you for your endless love, support and encouragement.

HarperCollins Publishers
77-85 Fulham Palace Road
London
W6 8JB

www.collins.co.uk

First published in 2006

12 11 10 09 08 07 06

10 9 8 7 6 5 4 3 2 1

0 00 720547 3

Editor: Emily Pitch
Commissioning Edi
Designer: Martin B
Proofreader: Claire
Index: Lisa Foottit

Colour reproductio
Printed and bound

CONTENTS

INTRODUCTION

There is something special about whales, dolphins and porpoises. They are still shrouded in mystery, yet the little we do know about them is both astonishing and awe-inspiring. They include the largest animal on Earth, the deepest-diving mammal, the mammal with the longest known migration, species that are capable of emitting the loudest sounds in nature, and many other extraordinary creatures. They also include some of the world's most critically endangered species.

Watching them in the wild is probably the ultimate wildlife experience. Once you have met a whale, dolphin or porpoise face-to-face, life is never quite the same again. There is an immense and lasting satisfaction in simply knowing that it is out there, wild and free. Who could ever forget the sight of a 50-tonne southern right whale launching itself high into the air, or of a sperm whale diving into the cold, dark depths hundreds or even thousands of metres below the surface? Who could fail to be intrigued

Short-beaked common dolphin, Sea of Cortez, Mexico

Southern right whales, Western Cape, South Africa

by Bahamonde's beaked whale, which is known from only
two partial skulls, an old tooth and a lower jaw, or remain
untouched by the plight of the last few surviving Yangtze
river dolphins?

It is not surprising that every year more than 10 million
people join organised whale and dolphin watching trips, in at
least 87 different countries and overseas territories around
the world.

The aim of this book is to introduce the world of whales,
dolphins and porpoises and to provide a handy pocket guide
for use in the field. It includes information on their evolution,
biology and natural history, describes how they are studied, the
threats they face, and some of the efforts to protect the ones
most in trouble. But most of all it provides a comprehensive
directory of all 84 currently-recognised species – and a few
more that could become distinct species in the future. I hope it
will help you to find, recognise, watch, enjoy and respect
whales, dolphins and porpoises in the wild.

THE NATURAL HISTORY OF WHALES, DOLPHINS AND PORPOISES

Evolution

The broad outline of the evolution of whales, dolphins and porpoises is quite well-known, but there are still many gaps in our knowledge. Tiny fragments – a few teeth or miniscule pieces of bone – sometimes provide the only tantalising clues to important links in their evolutionary chain.

They are believed to have evolved from a group of furry land mammals called mesonychids. These strange creatures looked rather like wolves, with four legs and a tail, but had hooves – so whales and hoofed animals such as hippos and deer appear to have a common ancestor. They lived around the ancient Tethys Sea, an area that is now the Mediterranean Sea and part of the Asian sub-continent, about 55–60 million years ago. The mesonychids probably

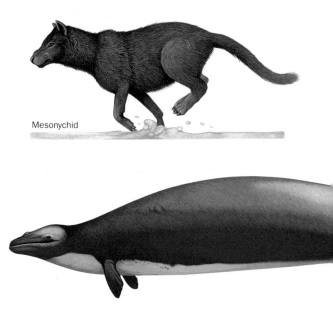

Mesonychid

spent their lives foraging for fish and other aquatic animals in coastal swamps and estuaries. As they spent more and more time in the water their bodies began to change. They became more streamlined and developed powerful, flattened tails; their forelimbs gradually turned into paddles and their hindlimbs wasted away; they developed insulating layers of fat and their body hair began to disappear; and, to help them breathe at the surface, their nostrils started to move towards the top of their heads to become blowholes.

It is still possible to see evidence of these land-based ancestors in modern whales, dolphins and porpoises. Intriguingly, the bone structure of the pectoral fin, or flipper, closely resembles an arm and hand with fingers; and, trapped inside the blubber, are the remains of pelvic bones that millions of years ago held their hindlimbs.

The first real whale-like animals appeared about 10 million years later. These ancient whales, or archaeocetes, spread rapidly throughout the oceans of the world – their fossilised remains have been found as far afield as Britain, Canada, Australia and even Antarctica. They were probably very similar to modern whales, dolphins and porpoises, although they were less well-adapted to life in the sea. They may even have clambered back onto land to breed, just like modern seals.

For reasons that are unclear the last of the archaeocetes probably died out about 25–30 million years ago but, by this time, representatives of more modern whales, dolphins and porpoises were fairly common and widespread. None were exactly the same as the species alive today, but they were unmistakably similar in appearance and way of life. The split between toothed whales (odontocetes) and baleen whales (mysticetes) occurred some 25–35 million years ago and by about five million years ago most, if not all, modern families of whales, dolphins and porpoises had become firmly established.

Archaeocete

Diversity

The sheer diversity of whales, dolphins and porpoises tends to surprise many people. A few species, such as the killer whale, narwhal and bottlenose dolphin, are relatively well-known. But the vast majority go unnoticed by all but the most dedicated whale-watchers.

In fact, there are currently no fewer than 84 recognised species altogether and, as research progresses, new discoveries continue to be made and the total count slowly but surely increases. A new species of beaked whale, Perrin's beaked whale, was formally recognised as recently as 2002 and the latest genetic research is revealing that some animals previously thought to be single species should actually be 'split'. In 1995, for example, the common dolphin was officially separated into two distinct species, now known as the short-beaked common dolphin and the long-beaked common dolphin. In the late 1990s, the minke whale was split into the common minke and the Antarctic minke and, in the future, it is possible that a third species – the dwarf minke – could be declared.

There is also some debate about Bryde's whales. A pygmy form will likely be assigned separate species status in the near future and, according to recent evidence from Japan, a third species is also possible. In the late 1970s, eight unidentified

Spinner dolphin, The Maldives

baleen whales were caught in the Indo-Pacific by Japanese whalers – and, in 1998, a ninth specimen was found beached on an island in the Sea of Japan. They all resembled fin whales, but were much smaller and had slightly unusual skulls and a different number of baleen plates. Genetic studies group all nine animals together as a single species, but separate them from all known baleen whale species.

While all these animals share many characteristics, there is no 'typical' whale, dolphin or porpoise. In size alone, they range from tiny dolphins and porpoises just over one metre long, to whales that are known to reach lengths of more than 33 metres. In terms of weight, the heaviest species is no less than 3,000 times heavier than the lightest.

They abound in an amazing variety of different shapes as well. Some are long and slender, others short and stocky. Some have huge dorsal fins, others have no fins at all. Many are brightly coloured or striking in black and white, while others are rather drab.

They also have a range of different habits and lifestyles. Some live in freezing cold waters near the poles, others prefer the warmer waters of the tropics. Many live in the middle of the deepest oceans, but others prefer to be much closer to shore, while a few even live hundreds of kilometres inland in rivers such as the Yangtze, the Ganges and the Amazon.

Humpback whale, Monterey Bay, USA

Is it a whale, a dolphin, or a porpoise?

Whales, dolphins and porpoises are known collectively as cetaceans. They form the largest of the three main groups of marine mammals surviving today, the others being the pinnipeds (seals, sea lions and walrus) and the sirenians (sea cows or manatees and dugong).

Interestingly, there is no real scientific basis for splitting cetaceans into the three groups commonly known as 'whales', 'dolphins' and 'porpoises'. Broadly speaking, the word 'whale' is used to describe the largest animals, 'dolphin' to describe the medium-sized ones, and 'porpoise' to describe the smallest. But this can be misleading, since some whales are smaller than the largest dolphins, and some dolphins are smaller than the largest porpoises.

There are many more confusing names and terms, as well. The rightwhale dolphins, for example, were named after right whales but are actually dolphins. At the same time, many are known by umpteen different names in at least as many different languages. Thus the northern giant bottlenose whale, North Pacific bottlenose whale, giant four-toothed whale, northern four-toothed whale and Baird's beaked whale are all the same species.

Melon-headed whales, The Maldives

Even more confusing are six members of the dolphin family, the Delphinidae, which have the word 'whale' in their names: killer whale, pygmy killer whale, false killer whale, melon-headed whale, long-finned pilot whale and short-finned pilot whale. These six species are often classified together in a group known as the 'blackfish', which is also rather strange since not all of them are black and, of course, none is a fish.

Scientists prefer to split modern cetaceans into just two distinct groups: the toothed whales, or Odontocetes, and the baleen whales, or Mysticetes. There was also a third group, known as the ancient whales or Archaeocetes, but all its members have been extinct for millions of years.

As their name suggests, the toothed whales possess teeth; this group of 71 species includes all the beaked whales, sperm whales, blackfish, oceanic dolphins, river dolphins and porpoises. The baleen whales make up the remaining 13 species and, instead of teeth, have hundreds of strange-looking baleen plates hanging down from their upper jaws; they make up for their lack of numbers by including most of the larger and better-known whales, including the blue, humpback, grey and right whales.

Inside and out

Whales, dolphins and porpoises are so streamlined, and so well adapted to life underwater, that they look rather like sharks and other large fish. They even have similar dorsal fins, flippers and powerful tails. But appearances can be deceptive. The similarities between them are simply the result of two unrelated groups of animals adapting in similar ways to identical living conditions. On closer inspection, there are actually more differences between them than there are similarities.

In particular, fish are cold-blooded, use their gills to extract all the oxygen they need directly from the water, and normally lay eggs or give birth to young that can feed themselves. In contrast, whales, dolphins and porpoises are mammals, like us, and so are warm-blooded, breathe air with lungs, and give birth to young that feed on their mother's milk for the first weeks or months of life.

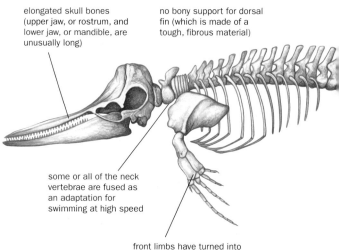

elongated skull bones (upper jaw, or rostrum, and lower jaw, or mandible, are unusually long)

no bony support for dorsal fin (which is made of a tough, fibrous material)

some or all of the neck vertebrae are fused as an adaptation for swimming at high speed

front limbs have turned into flippers, or pectoral fins, yet the original structure of the arm, hand and finger bones is still visible

One of the most striking features of any cetacean is the thick layer of insulating fat under the skin, known as blubber, which they have instead of hair or fur. This helps them to keep warm in water, which sucks heat out of a mammal up to 25 times faster than in air.

A detailed look inside their bodies reveals many other interesting features and adaptations for their underwater life:

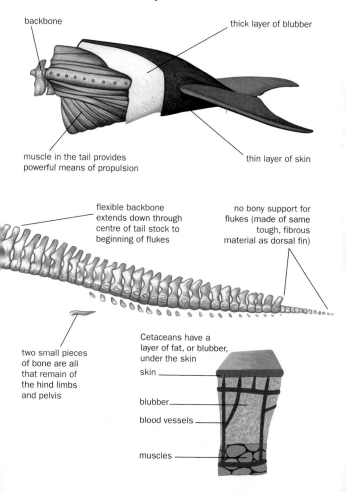

backbone

thick layer of blubber

muscle in the tail provides powerful means of propulsion

thin layer of skin

flexible backbone extends down through centre of tail stock to beginning of flukes

no bony support for flukes (made of same tough, fibrous material as dorsal fin)

two small pieces of bone are all that remain of the hind limbs and pelvis

Cetaceans have a layer of fat, or blubber, under the skin

skin

blubber

blood vessels

muscles

Diving and swimming

The fastest speed ever achieved by a human swimmer is an incredible 8.64 km/h by American Tom Jager, on 23 March 1990 in Nashville, USA. Equally impressive, the record depth attained for no-limits freediving is 209 metres, achieved by Belgian Patrick Musimu on 30 June 2005, in the Red Sea. And on 8 November 2003, Frenchman Stephane Mifsud held his breath for a record-breaking eight minutes 24 seconds.

But these superhuman feats barely register on the scale of the swimming and diving records achieved by whales, dolphins and porpoises. Killer whales, Dall's porpoises and several other species have been clocked at speeds of up to 55 km/h, while sperm whales (and, possibly, some beaked whales) can dive to depths of at least 2,000 metres and have been known to stay underwater for nearly two hours at a time.

All cetaceans are proficient swimmers and divers, even though they breathe air and, consequently, have to hold their breath whenever they disappear underwater. Their lungs are relatively small, but they are able to extract much more oxygen from the air than human lungs and then use it far more efficiently.

Killer whales, Monterey Bay, western USA

Avoiding the 'bends': Human scuba divers can suffer from a potentially fatal condition known as decompression sickness, or the 'bends'. It is caused by nitrogen bubbling out of the blood, either when the divers stay down for too long or when they rise to the surface too quickly. These bubbles then lodge in joints and cause severe pain, or in vital blood vessels and cause paralysis or even death.

Marine biologists have always assumed that cetaceans are immune to the bends, but now it seems that rising to the surface too quickly from deep water may be just as dangerous for them as it is for us. Damage consistent with decompression sickness has been found in the bones of sperm whales and beaked whales.

Humpback whale, Silver Bank, Dominican Republic

Avoiding 'nitrogen narcosis': On deep dives, human scuba divers can suffer from another dangerous condition called 'nitrogen narcosis'. They start losing control over what they are doing and their judgement begins to deteriorate, as if they are drunk. In a way, they behave like car drivers under the influence of alcohol because, although nitrogen narcosis is not dangerous in itself, it makes accidents far more likely.

Whales, dolphins and porpoises do not suffer from nitrogen narcosis either, because it is induced by breathing nitrogen under pressure – and they breathe it only at the surface.

Food and feeding

Most whales, dolphins and porpoises feed on fish, squid or crustaceans, but some will take a wide variety of other prey as well – at virtually every level in the marine ecosystem – ranging from octopuses to other large whales.

Between them, they have an astonishing range of different hunting techniques. For example, killer whales in Patagonia will beach themselves to catch sea lion pups; strap-toothed whales suck squid into their mouths so quickly that the squid appear to have been attached to pieces of invisible elastic; belugas blast powerful jets of water to dislodge fish hiding in mud on the seabed; open-ocean dolphins work together to corral fish against the surface of the sea; and blue whales take huge quantities of water into their mouths, and then filter out as much as four tonnes of shrimp-like krill every day.

In turn, they themselves are preyed upon by large sharks and even by some of their own kind: killer whales, false killer whales and pygmy killer whales. The smaller species are most at risk, but no whale is too large for a determined pod of killer whales.

Teeth: As their name suggests, all toothed whales have teeth. But the number varies greatly from species to species and, in some female beaked whales, they have no visible teeth at all (they do not erupt). Cetacean teeth come in a variety of shapes and sizes, but in most cases each species has just one design – in other words, they are not differentiated into incisors, canines, pre-molars and molars. Unlike other mammals, toothed whales do not have two sets of teeth, but retain their first set for life.

Sperm whale   Ginkgo-toothed   Fraser's
                 beaked whale   Dolphin

Baleen plates: Instead of teeth, most large whales have hundreds of strange-looking structures hanging down from their upper jaws. These are called baleen plates. They overlap one another, inside the mouth, to form bristly sieves for filtering small animals out of the seawater. Some 400–700 baleen plates is typical for most whales, but their number, size and shape varies greatly from species to species.

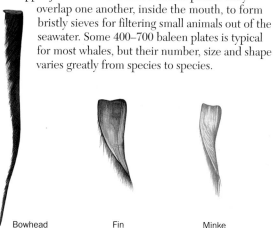

Bowhead   Fin   Minke

Krill: Krill are small, shrimp-like crustaceans, known in the scientific world as euphausiids. Full of protein, and living in dense swarms, they make ideal food for large whales. There are at least 80 different species of krill, ranging in length from eight to 60 millimetres, but perhaps the most important is the five- to six-centimetre Antarctic krill. This is the staple food of all baleen whales in the Antarctic, as well as fish, squid, penguins and seals.

Migration

Many large baleen whales have little choice but to split their year into four distinct parts. They spend a few months, in the summer, gorging themselves on schooling fish and krill, in high-latitude, cold water feeding grounds; in the autumn, they migrate to low-latitude, warm water breeding grounds; then they spend a few months, during the winter, mating and calving; and finally, in the spring, they migrate all the way back to their feeding grounds, and the annual cycle begins all over again.

The problem they face is that most of their food is in colder regions, in temperate latitudes and towards the sub-Arctic and the Antarctic. In an ideal world, this is where they would live year-round. Unfortunately, though, the food is only present in large quantities during the summer and, even if they stayed for the winter to breed, their newborn calves may not be able to survive the freezing cold temperatures. In other words, their preferred feeding and breeding grounds can be thousands of kilometres apart.

Short-finned pilot whale, western USA

Researchers studying whale migration have made some incredible discoveries in recent years. Some humpback whales, for example, swim between their feeding grounds near the Antarctic Peninsula and their breeding grounds off the coast of Colombia every year – an astonishing round-trip of 17,400 kilometres. Another humpback whale was recorded swimming all the way across the North Pacific, from south-east Alaska to Hawaii, in just 39 days.

But in most cases the more subtle details of their migrations are still a mystery. How do they know when to leave, and when to return? How do they find their way? Do they stop to rest, or feed? Do they swim near the surface, or travel at depth? There are so many unanswered questions.

Not all large baleen whales undertake these extensive migrations. Many Bryde's and minke whales are able to live in non-extreme temperatures year-round, while sei whales, and some humpbacks and greys, do not bother to complete their journeys if they find adequate food supplies en route. Fin whales in Mexico's Sea of Cortez, and blue whales in the northern Indian Ocean, seem to be permanent residents, while bowhead whales simply move backwards and forwards in their high Arctic home, with the advancing and retreating ice.

Blue whale, Sea of Cortez, Mexico

Regular long-distance migrations are virtually unknown in toothed whales, with one major exception. While female and young sperm whales spend most of their lives in warm waters, many of the older males are believed to move to rich feeding grounds, in high-latitude cold waters, during the spring and summer.

Reproduction and social life

There are almost as many different reproductive strategies
and ways of living together as there are species of whales,
dolphins and porpoises. But it is a difficult field of research,
and we are only just beginning to learn about the private
lives of some better-known species.

Sexual maturity: The age of sexual maturity varies greatly
from species to species. At one extreme, male sperm whales
are not sexually mature until they are about 18–21 years old;
even then, they often have to wait another few years before
they are big and strong enough to gain access to receptive
females. At the other extreme, female harbour porpoises
reach sexual maturity at about three years old and begin to
breed the following year. After reaching breeding age, the
females of many species spend their entire adult lives
either with a calf by their side or a foetus growing inside
them – or both.

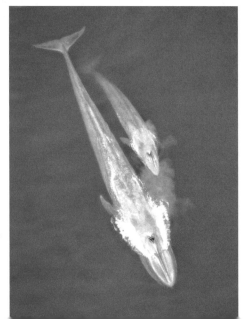

Blue whale
mother and
calf, Sea
of Cortez,
Mexico

Courtship and mating: Courtship and mating can be long and involved affairs, with leaping, games of chase, touching and caressing for several hours before the two animals join together, belly to belly, although the details vary greatly from one species to another. In some species, such as humpback whales, there can be intense competition and serious fighting between males battling over access to females. There are no records of cetaceans being monogamous – it has never been known for one male to mate exclusively with one female. In the sperm whale, beaked whales and some other species, one male mates with many females; but, in most species, they are believed to be promiscuous: each individual mates with numerous other individuals of the opposite sex.

Gestation period: The gestation period is unknown for many cetaceans, but seems to range from about eight months in some porpoises to at least 16 months in sperm whales; there is a possible record of 18 months 28 days for one particular sperm whale. Surprisingly, it is not dependent on body size: in the blue whale, for example, it is roughly 11–12 months, whereas in the much smaller narwhal it is at least 14 months.

Birth: Few cetacean births have been witnessed in captivity, and even fewer in the wild, but we are gradually building up a reasonable picture of what happens. Like most mammals, whales, dolphins and porpoises give birth to live young, although they normally have just one at a time. The calves are born underwater, near the surface where it is easier for them to catch their first breath, and their eyes are already open. They are able to swim, albeit a little awkwardly, almost as soon as they enter the water. The calves are virtually identical to their parents, although their dorsal fins and tail flukes are more rubbery and they do not have baleen or teeth (which begin to erupt when they are a few weeks old). They are normally about a third of the length of their mothers; a newborn blue whale, for example, is an incredible seven metres long and weighs some three tonnes in total.

Nursing: It is believed that the father plays no active role in caring for the calf, so it is the mother's responsibility alone. Suckling takes place underwater, and she literally squirts her rich, fat-laden milk into the young animal's mouth. The calf grows quickly. A young blue whale, for example, grows almost four centimetres and gains 90 kilograms every day – equivalent to the weight of an average adult man. Weaning is usually gradual, with a period of overlap when the calf is drinking milk and eating solid food at the same time. It stays with its mother for weeks, months or even years afterwards, depending on the species. In general, toothed whales tend to have fewer young and look after them for a relatively long time, whereas baleen whales have more young and look after them for a relatively short time.

Lifespan: It is difficult to assess the ages of whales, dolphins and porpoises accurately and the maximum lifespan for most species is unknown. However, the limited information available suggests that the larger whales tend to have the longest lifespans – probably well in excess of 100 years in the bowhead whale and some others. Certain dolphins and porpoises may have an average life-expectancy of less than 20 years. The two main natural causes of death are predation and disease. A variety of accidents and, of course, human-induced deaths also take their toll.

Social life: Whales, dolphins and porpoises often have complex social lives and have adopted many different ways of living together. Some prefer to live alone, or in small groups, while others roam the seas in the company of hundreds or thousands of their contemporaries. Historically, there are even records of dolphin schools at least 100,000-strong. Some species, such as killer whales and long-finned pilot whales, live in groups that are stable for many years – they remain together for the entire lives of the individuals in them. Others are incredibly fluid and their membership changes all the time, with individuals coming and going quite freely. Often, the membership of a group will vary according to specific requirements on a day-by-day or even hour-by-hour basis.

Commonly asked questions

How intelligent are they?

Are whales, dolphins and porpoises as intelligent as we would like to believe? They certainly *seem* to be intelligent: they have large brains, frequently live in complex societies, help one another in times of trouble, learn from experience, are often playful, and sometimes even seem to enjoy human company. But, in truth, no one really knows. Some people claim that they are no more intelligent than cats and dogs, while others go so far as to say that they may be our intellectual superiors.

There are two main reasons for this confusion. The first lies in defining what we mean by 'intelligent' and then taking meaningful measurements. Many definitions have been proposed over the years, but intelligence is broadly considered to be an ability to learn from experience and then to analyse new situations, rather than simply reacting to

Friendly bottlenose dolphin with swimmer, Kaikoura, New Zealand

them. In other words, intelligent animals are able to *solve* problems by grasping fundamental principles, and then making considered judgements, rather than fumbling around trying to get things right by trial and error. Even with an acceptable definition, though, obtaining accurate measurements is another matter altogether. It is hard enough in humans, because the results can be frustratingly ambiguous and difficult to understand. But it is even more challenging in other animals, which cannot talk or work with tools such as pens or computers.

The second reason is that any discussion of intelligence tends to be highly subjective. After all, we have only a human perspective, and can scarcely imagine what goes on inside another animal's mind. Even by saying that a whale or dolphin is more intelligent than, say, a rat or a chicken, we impose a very egocentric set of values and rules.

The simple fact that whales, dolphins and porpoises have embarked on a completely different evolutionary path from our own makes any comparison almost impossible. Human intelligence suits our own way of life and, consequently, a large part of our brain deals with the use of hands to write, paint, sculpt, build or manipulate objects that exist outside our own bodies.

If we were to judge whales and dolphins on these terms, they would fare badly. But their intelligence suits a completely different way of life, and may concentrate instead on social skills, emotional self-control and other more spiritual and philosophical requirements. Taking this into consideration, many people would argue that whales and dolphins are far more intelligent in their world than we are in ours. But the jury is still out.

Why do they strand?

Every year, hundreds or even thousands of whales, dolphins and porpoises are found stranded on coastlines all over the world. They may be alive or dead, alone or in groups, and healthy or unwell. These strandings are believed to be a natural phenomenon (although, in modern times, pollution and acoustic disturbance may be contributory causes in some areas) and have probably been happening for thousands of years. But *why* they happen remains one of the great unsolved mysteries of the animal kingdom.

Strandings of dead animals are relatively easy to explain – they simply die at sea and are washed ashore with the tides and currents – and live animals often strand because they are very ill. But mass strandings of otherwise healthy animals are more baffling. Many theories have been suggested, ranging from severe weather (quite possible) to mass suicide bids (highly unlikely).

But recent research implies that it could be storms exploding from the sun that are making the whales run aground. Historical records of sperm whales found beached in the North Sea, over a 300-year period, show an amazing match with the number of 'sunspots' that blast electrical energy into space. This smashes into the earth's magnetic field (which the whales may use for navigation) and disrupts their internal compasses.

In reality, of course, there may be different explanations for different strandings, depending on the species, location and a variety of other factors.

Stranded sperm whale,
Horta, Faial, The Azores

What should you do if you find a stranded animal?

Without human intervention, when a live whale, dolphin or porpoise strands it usually dies. Cetaceans are not adapted to life on land – they quickly overheat and, out of the relatively weightless medium of the sea, their light bones cannot support their bodies and they literally crush themselves to death. Rescuing a stranded animal is extremely difficult and normally requires great skill and patience. Well-intentioned, but misdirected, efforts can cause considerable stress to the animal and may even result in its death. It can also be quite dangerous to attempt a rescue, since even small cetaceans have been known to injure human helpers when they thrash around. Perhaps not surprisingly, in some countries it is illegal to give unauthorised first aid to any stranded cetacean.

These very basic guidelines are designed merely to make a stranded animal as comfortable as possible until expert help arrives. The golden rule in every case is to call the local police immediately and to attempt a rescue yourself only if expert help is unavailable.

■ Try to keep the animal upper-side up, taking care not to trap either of the flippers under its body, and never pushing or pulling on the flippers, flukes or head.

■ Keep the animal's skin moist and cool, with wet towels or water, but be careful not to cover the blowhole (or to let either water or sand enter the blowhole).

■ Erect a shelter to provide shade from the sun, but never apply suntan lotion to the animal's skin.

■ Keep onlookers and their dogs at a distance, make as little noise as possible, and do not touch the animal more than necessary.

■ Never, under any circumstances, attempt to destroy a stranded animal yourself.

Spinner dolphin which died
after stranding,
Sri Lanka

How do they sleep?

The way in which whales, dolphins and porpoises sleep has
baffled and intrigued scientists for a very long time. Aristotle
seemed particularly excited, centuries ago, when he noted
that 'there are even people who have heard a dolphin snore'.

Over the years, of course, there have been some
interesting theories. One was that they haul themselves out
of the sea after dark and then spend the night curled up on
shore in the company of seals and sea lions; no-one had
actually seen them doing it, but the idea probably seemed
quite logical at the time. Another theory was that they simply
dive down to the seabed, make themselves comfortable, and
lie there for the night.

In fact, the truth is even stranger than the fiction. Unlike
most other mammals, cetaceans never fall into a deep sleep,
and they do not seem to have regular sleeping patterns
linked to night and day. They do sleep, of course, though not
in the way we might expect.

The reason is simple. Since our breathing is automatic, we can safely sleep and breathe at the same time. But cetaceans control their breathing consciously, so they have to be awake, and able to think, in order to take regular breaths. If they were to fall into a deep sleep, which is a naturally-occurring state of unconsciousness, they would then drown.

Keiko, a captive killer whale used in the *Free Willy* films, Oregon, USA

Instead of long periods of deep sleep, their solution is to swim along slowly, or lie just below the surface, and take short 'cat-naps'. They are believed to go into a semi-conscious state by switching off one half of the brain at a time. Then they swap sides to ensure that both halves are fully rested. While one side of the brain is asleep, the other remains awake to control the breathing and, of course, to look out for predators.

Should they be kept in captivity?

During the past century, more than 25 species of whales, dolphins and porpoises have been kept in captivity in zoos, marine parks and aquaria around the world. Thousands of individual animals have been captured in the wild, sometimes for research or military purposes, but mainly to perform special shows for the fee-paying public. They are trained to jump through hoops, balance balls on their heads, 'kiss' their trainers, perform somersaults and synchronised leaps, and to do many other tricks for the millions of people who flock to see them every year.

Their owners argue that the animals 'enjoy' the shows, and are fortunate to be safe from predators, pollution and other threats in the wild. They point out that, as the undisputed stars of zoos and marine parks, they are worth a great deal of money and, directly or indirectly, provide thousands of people with secure jobs. They also claim that captive animals encourage members of the public to take an interest in the conservation of their wild relatives.

Some facilities are obviously much better than others, and whales and dolphins are kept in a bewildering range of establishments, from dirty hotel pools to professional marine parks with large, coastal enclosures that are filled naturally with seawater and flushed with every new tide. Many of the animals are treated abominably, while a very lucky few receive the best care and attention that money can buy.

But most conservation and animal welfare groups are strongly opposed to keeping whales, dolphins or porpoises in captivity of any kind. They say that it is immoral and cruel. Taken from the wild, and separated from their well-structured family groups, the animals are often forced to live alone or with unfamiliar species. Many of them are kept in small and featureless concrete tanks, where they can no longer hunt or hear the sounds of the sea, and may even be deprived of natural sunlight. At the same time, they have to eat dead fish and cope with hordes of noisy people watching them day after day.

To make matters worse, few zoos or marine parks make a genuine effort to educate the public, or 'educate' them with inaccurate information, so the real benefits and spin-offs for their wild relatives are very limited. At the end of the day, there is little doubt that most captive animals are there simply to provide cheap entertainment for profit.

Will we ever be able to talk to them?

Whales, dolphins and porpoises are known to communicate in two main ways: by sound and with body language. They may even be telepathic, as well, and thus able to communicate without speech or movement.

But current evidence suggests that they probably do not have a true language. While they can pass on information such as danger, irritation or sexual interest, they probably cannot complain about the poor size of fish, discuss the vagaries of the weather, or talk about their plans for the future. In other words, they can give simple commands and signals, but probably cannot discuss more abstract concepts.

However, there is no doubt that we still have a great deal to learn about their communication skills. Some dolphins, for example, seem to have their own 'signature whistles', which are almost the equivalent of human names. They use these to attract the attention of other dolphins and to identify themselves; there is even some evidence to suggest that one dolphin will call the name of another in its group.

In captivity, research also demonstrates that they can grasp the essential elements of any human language. They do not actually speak, of course, but they can respond correctly to sentences up to five words long. This suggests that they have the *potential* to develop a language, even if they have not done so in the wild.

Humpback whale watchers, eastern USA

Whether or not we will ever be able to communicate with them is another matter altogether. In the past, people predicted that we would be conversing with dolphins, and other small cetaceans, within a few decades; others went so far as to suggest that if an alien intelligence were to attempt to communicate with life on Earth, it might choose dolphins in preference to humans. But these are dreams that have yet to come true.

How do they find their way around?

Whales, dolphins and porpoises find their way around their underwater world in ways that are well beyond the scope of our own senses. Most of them retain the senses of sight, touch and taste, but they rely mainly on hearing. They are also believed to have an extra sense, known as geomagnetism, which enables them to detect the Earth's magnetic field.

Killer whale, northern Norway

The ability to see varies greatly from one species to another. While some of the river dolphins are virtually blind, for example, most marine cetaceans can see fairly well in both air and water. However, sight is of limited benefit to them since they spend so much of their lives in the dark depths or in turbid water where visibility is poor even close to the surface.

Hearing is far more important. Effective at night as well as during the day, it does not rely on good visibility. Sound travels through water nearly five times faster than through air and can be heard over much longer distances. Although cetaceans have lost the distinctive outer ear flaps typical of most other mammals, they do have ears in the form of tiny holes in the skin behind their eyes. Many species can probably also receive sounds through their lower jaws.

The senses of taste and smell are very similar, because they are both used to detect chemicals. It is possible to smell underwater: sharks, for example, can smell chemicals in the water from a long distance away. But toothed whales have probably lost their sense of smell altogether, and baleen whales retain only a rudimentary form – mainly because their nostrils (or blowholes) have to remain tightly shut when they dive. Taste is far more important and is used for detecting chemicals both inside and near the outside of the mouth.

Whales, dolphins and porpoises also have very sensitive skin and are able to use their dorsal fins, flippers and beaks to investigate unfamiliar objects, and to touch one another as a form of greeting, or to strengthen social bonds.

Geomagnetism is undoubtedly the least known of all the senses. It involves detecting or 'reading' the Earth's magnetic field, possibly using it like an invisible 'map' to navigate over large distances. Many animals, from bacteria and bees to reptiles and birds, are believed to have this sixth sense. It may even exist to a limited degree in humans – what we identify in ourselves simply as a 'sense of direction'. But it seems to be particularly well developed in many cetaceans, and may help them to navigate their way across the world's seas and oceans.

Whales and dolphins are believed to 'read' the Earth's magnetic field like an invisible 'map'.

What is echolocation?

Most whales, dolphins and porpoises have a remarkable sensory system, called echolocation, which enables them to build up a 'picture' of their underwater surroundings with the help of sound. Bats, shrews, cave swiftlets, oilbirds and a number of other land-based animals use a similar system to hunt fast-moving prey in the dark.

The basic principle of the echolocation system used by cetaceans is quite simple: they transmit ultrasonic clicks into the water, and then monitor and interpret any echoes that bounce back. The clicks are believed to be produced within the nasal plugs, or in the larynx, and are then focused into a directional beam by the fatty 'melon' (which appears as a rounded forehead on most species). The returning echoes may be picked up by the small ear holes on either side of the head, but recent research suggests that they are more likely to be transmitted to the brain via the lower jaw.

Common dolphin, Mexico

Echolocation is actually a form of sonar (radar works in a similar way, but uses electromagnetic radiation instead of sound). However, the system used by many cetaceans is so complex and sophisticated that it leaves human sonar experts gasping: the human system, although useful, is little more than a crude imitation by comparison. When homing in on a fish, for example, a dolphin can use echolocation to identify the fish's size and shape, which way it is swimming, its texture, and possibly even its internal structure.

Toothed whales are the real echolocation experts. They use it for keeping track of one another, navigating around objects in the water, identifying changes in sea-floor profile, hunting, and monitoring the surroundings for potential predators or prey. It is even possible that some toothed whales may be able to use particularly powerful blasts of ultrasonic clicks to stun or kill their prey. Baleen whales may also be able to echolocate, but this has never been proven and any sonar system they do have is probably much less well-developed. How baleen whales find their food is still largely a mystery.

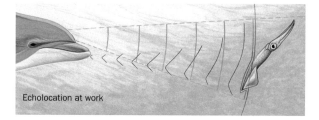

Echolocation at work

Record-breakers

Largest: The blue whale is the largest animal on Earth. The average adult length is 25 metres in males and 26.2 metres in females, with body weights of 90–120 tonnes. The heaviest ever recorded was a female, caught in the Southern Ocean on 20 March 1947, which weighed 190 tonnes. The longest ever recorded was another female, landed in 1909 at Grytviken, South Georgia, in the South Atlantic, which measured 33.58 metres from the tip of her snout to the end of her tail.

Blue whale, Sea of Cortez, Mexico

Smallest: It is very difficult to identify the world's smallest cetacean, partly because there is so much variation between individuals. Taking the maximum known length as a guide, it is a competition between Hector's dolphin (1.38 metres for the smaller male) and the vaquita (1.45 metres also for the smaller male).

Longest flippers: The longest flippers belong to the humpback whale. They grow to 23–31 per cent of the length of the whale – making a potential maximum of over 5.5 metres – but typically measure around 4.6 metres in fully grown animals. They are used to herd fish, to manoeuvre while swimming, to comfort their young and to slap the surface of the water.

Humpback whale, New England, USA

Tallest dorsal fin: The huge, triangular dorsal fin of the bull killer whale can reach a remarkable height of 1.8 metres, which makes it roughly as tall as a man. In comparison, the blue whale's dorsal fin is relatively small, rarely reaching more than 40 centimetres in height.

Longest baleen plate: The longest baleen is found in the bowhead whale. There are many records within the three to four metre range, but lengths of up to 5.18 metres have been reported for animals killed during the nineteenth century.

Longest tooth: The male narwhal has two teeth. The one on the right normally remains invisible, but the one on the left grows to a remarkable length. It pierces the animal's upper lip, develops into a long tusk and eventually looks rather like a gnarled and twisted walking stick. At least a third of all narwhal tusks are broken, but unbroken tusks reach an average length of about two metres. In extreme cases, they have been known to exceed three metres and weigh more than 10 kilograms.

Bowhead whale, Nunavut, Arctic Canada

Thickest blubber: The blubber of the bowhead whale is thicker than in any other animal, averaging an incredible 43–50 centimetres. It provides the whale with protection against the freezing cold waters of its Arctic home.

Tallest blow: The 'blow' or 'spout' is the cloud of condensed air and water droplets produced above a whale's head when it blows out. The tallest blow is made by the blue whale: slender and vertical in shape, it can reach an astonishing height of 15 metres – which is clearly visible from several kilometres away.

Fastest: On 12 October 1958, a bull killer whale was timed swimming at 55.5 km/h in the eastern North Pacific. Similar speeds, albeit in short bursts, have also been reported for Dall's porpoises.

Largest appetite: The largest blue whales probably eat as much as 5.5 tonnes of small shrimp-like creatures, called krill, every day. Even an average-sized blue whale is believed to eat about four tonnes. Since each of these tiny animals weighs only about one gramme, a daily intake of about four million of them is required to keep the whale going. In terms of weight, this is equivalent to eating a fully-grown African elephant every day. The whale does not feed year-round, but gorges itself all summer and then fasts during the winter.

Largest prey: Killer whales have been known to prey on more than 25 different whale and dolphin species – and there have been several reported attacks on sperm whales and blues. The largest giant squid known to be taken by a sperm whale was 14.5 metres long, including its tentacles; it was caught on Great Bahama Bank, in the Bahamas.

Noisiest: The low-frequency booms made by blue whales and fin whales when vocalising across enormous stretches of ocean have been measured at up to 188 decibels, making them the loudest sounds emitted by any living source. These remarkable sounds are below the range of human hearing, but with the right equipment they can be detected over distances of up to 3,000 kilometres. It is not yet clear whether they are for long-distance communication or are part of a long-range sonar navigation system for detecting underwater features such as seamounts.

Longest-lived: It is difficult to measure the age of a whale accurately, so the maximum lifespan is not known for most species. However, indirect evidence suggests that some of the larger whales, at least, are able to reach a grand old age of considerably more than 100 years. In 1995, a freshly-killed bowhead whale was being processed in Alaska when the Inuit hunters found two stone harpoon blades embedded in its blubber. Since the use of these particular harpoons ended a century ago, the animal must have been at least 100 years old – and might have survived a lot longer if it had not been killed by people. Meanwhile, scientists have developed a way

Fin whale, New England, USA

of determining the ages of some whales by examining the amino acids in the lenses of their eyes. Limited evidence from this research suggests that another bowhead whale in Alaska may have been 211 years old when killed.

Shortest-lived: The lifespan for many small cetaceans, in particular, is unknown and it is very difficult to be certain of the shortest. One possible contender is Burmeister's porpoise, which has not been known to live beyond 12 years. But this is a poorly-known species and future research may increase this figure.

Longest migration: Humpback whales are inveterate travellers and their migrations are phenomenal – the longest known of any mammal. In 1990, for example, one particular humpback was identified by American biologists off the Antarctic Peninsula; less then five months later, it was

Sperm whales, Sea of Cortez, Mexico

identified by Colombian biologists off their own coast, north of the equator. It had travelled almost 8,700 kilometres. Since then, several other humpbacks have been identified in both Antarctica and Colombia, confirming that the first individual was not simply lost.

Deepest diver: Sperm whales can dive for longer than two hours to depths of at least 2,000 metres and probably deeper.

Most acrobatic: Many whales, dolphins and porpoises are known for their aerial displays. Among the larger species, right whales, humpback whales and killer whales are particularly acrobatic. Humpbacks have been known to leap almost clear of the water more than 80 times in a row – which is a phenomenal achievement considering an average-sized humpback weighs the equivalent of 400 people. There are also many outstanding acrobats in the dolphin family. Bottlenose, spotted, striped, dusky and other dolphins have been known to hurl themselves as high as seven metres into the air and frequently turn somersaults before re-entering the water. But perhaps the most spectacular acrobat is the spinner dolphin, which leaps high into the air, then spins around on its longitudinal axis as many as seven times before splashing back into the water.

Most contaminated: Belugas living in the Gulf of St Lawrence, Canada, are so badly contaminated with heavy metals, organochlorines and benzoapyrene that, when they die, their bodies could qualify as toxic waste.

Most studied: A number of individual whales and dolphins have been studied in the wild for many years. One of the most studied is a female humpback whale called Salt. She was first sighted on 1 May 1976 by biologists studying the whales around Stellwagen Bank, off the coast of New England, USA. She has been observed and photographed by dozens of scientists, and thousands of whale-watchers, around Stellwagen Bank and nearby Jeffery's Ledge every summer since. Salt has also been studied in her Caribbean breeding grounds for many years, since she was first sighted off the coast of the Dominican Republic in 1978.

CONSERVATION

Endangered species

To the best of our knowledge, no whale, dolphin or porpoise has become extinct in modern times (although no one is certain about the status of the Yangtze river dolphin, or baiji). But a frightening number are in serious trouble, and others have all but disappeared from many of their former haunts.

Considering the magnitude of the problems they face, the odds are firmly stacked against them and, for some at least, the future is undoubtedly bleak.

It is difficult to judge which species is the most endangered. Unfortunately, our knowledge is so inadequate that there are no widely accepted population estimates for the vast majority. Several beaked whales, for example, are known only from stranded specimens and have never been seen alive – but the total lack of observations in the wild does not necessarily mean they are rare, especially since few beaked whales are seen

Some of the rarest whales, dolphins and porpoises in the world

	SPECIES	DISTRIBUTION
1	Yangtze river dolphin or baiji	Yangtze river, China (middle and lower reaches)
2	North Atlantic and North Pacific right whales	North Atlantic and North Pacific
3	Vaquita or Gulf of California porpoise	Extreme northern end of the Gulf of California (Sea of Cortez), Mexico
4	Indus river dolphin	Main channel of the Indus river, Pakistan, downstream of Chashma Barrage
5	Hector's dolphin	Coastal waters of New Zealand (most common around South Island)

regularly. At the same time, the number of survivors is not the only consideration. The blue whale, for example, is not one of the rarest cetaceans in the world but, after decades of intensive whaling, its chances of recovery are severely limited because it is a particularly slow breeder and because its obliterated population is widely dispersed.

The table below summarises five of the rarest whales, dolphins and porpoises for which population figures are known. Of course, it is possible that some poorly-known species are even rarer than the ones on this list.

Yangtze river dolphin, Wuhan, China

Population	Notes
Likely to be in the low tens or extinct	Now very little chance of rescuing this species, which is likely to become the first cetacean known to become extinct
300 in the North Atlantic; a few hundred in the North Pacific	Hunted almost to extinction by commercial whalers and has never recovered
Fewer than 600	Has the most restricted distribution of any marine cetacean; most commonly seen around the Colorado river delta
Fewer than 1,000	The many threats to its survival include pollution, hunting, fishing and dam construction
Fewer than 3,000	Threatened mainly by entanglement in coastal gillnets (may have reduced population by 50 per cent since 1970)

Whaling

Coastal communities around the world have killed whales for centuries. The blubber and meat provides a welcome source of light, heat and food that is sometimes essential for human survival.

In the old days, this small-scale subsistence hunting probably had only a local impact on whale populations, but by the end of the seventeenth century the character of whaling had changed beyond all recognition. In an age before petroleum or plastics, whales provided valuable raw materials for thousands of everyday products, from soap and candles to whips and corsets. There were huge profits to be made and whaling rapidly became big business.

The slaughter reached its worst excesses around the middle of this century, thanks largely to a series of technological advances in whaling vessels, killing equipment and processing methods. In 1930–31, for example, a record 30,000 blue whales were killed, and in 1963–64, no fewer than 29,255 sperm whales were killed.

Indigenous whaling in the Caribbean

One by one the great whales were hunted almost to the point of extinction. In the space of a few hundred years, literally millions of them were killed around the world. Today, we are left merely with the tattered remains: in most cases, no more than five to 10 per cent of their original populations. There are barely 300 surviving North Atlantic right whales, the bowhead has all but disappeared from vast areas of its former range, and so the catalogue of destruction unfolds. During the twentieth century, more than two million whales were killed in the southern hemisphere alone.

Yet, incredibly, we still have not learnt the lessons of the past. The story of commercial whaling continues as Norway, Iceland and Japan persist in hunting whales in the north Atlantic, the north Pacific and the Antarctic. In blatant defiance of world opinion, they are gradually expanding their activities and, alarmingly, they are being watched with considerable interest by other nations that may ultimately decide to resume whaling themselves.

To make matters even worse, it is virtually impossible to kill whales humanely. In some cases, it can take as long as an hour for them to die agonising deaths after explosive harpoons have blown huge, gaping holes in their bodies. As one ex-whaler commented: 'If whales could scream, whaling would have stopped many years ago'.

Commercial whaling in Iceland

The Faroese pilot whale hunt

Large whales are not the only cetaceans to suffer from hunting. It is believed that tens of thousands of small whales, dolphins and porpoises are killed every year in seas and oceans around the world, although the true extent of the problem is unknown. Nets, knives, rifles, hand-held harpoons and even explosive harpoons are used for the killing.

One of the most controversial of these hunts takes place in the Faroes, a group of islands lying halfway between Scotland and Iceland in the north-east Atlantic. Entire pods of long-finned pilot whales (as well as several dolphin species caught up in the hunt incidentally) are herded into sandy bays by men in small boats, during noisy 'drives' that frequently take many hours to complete. All the animals – including pregnant and lactating females and their babies – are dragged ashore with steel hooks, called gaffs, and then killed with long knives.

Faroese hunting statistics date back to 1584, with unbroken records from 1709 to the present day. During this most recent 295-year period, more than a quarter of a million long-finned pilot whales have been killed in approximately 1,700 different drives. The official number of whales taken each year ranges from zero to a peak of 4,385 recorded in 1941. An average of around 1,200 whales have been taken each year during the past decade.

The Faroese defend the hunt vigorously, arguing that it is a traditional part of their culture and provides a free and welcome source of protein. But opponents of the hunt argue that it is terribly cruel and no longer necessary in such a modern society with a relatively high standard of living; they also argue that no one knows enough about the number of pilot whales around the Faroes, their wider distribution and movements throughout the year, or any of the other dangers they face, to judge whether or not the hunt is a threat to their future survival.

Ironically, recent evidence suggests that it may actually be dangerous to eat long-finned pilot whales taken from the north Atlantic. Their meat and blubber have been found to contain high levels of toxic chemicals and could seriously threaten the health of the Faroese people. At the same time, of course, the presence of so many pollutants inevitably raises concern about the fitness of the whales themselves.

Whale meat drying in the Faroe Islands

Conflicts with fisheries

Since the 1950s, the staggering growth of many modern fisheries and the introduction of increasingly destructive fishing methods have spelt disaster for whales, dolphins and porpoises around the world.

Hundreds of thousands of them – possibly millions – die slow, lingering deaths in fishing nets every year. Many more could be threatened by the sheer scale of modern fisheries, which over-exploit fish stocks with scant regard for the future health of the world's oceans. And in some parts of the world fishermen intentionally kill cetaceans and other marine mammals, either to use as bait or because they view them as competition for 'their' fish. Not surprisingly, few scientists are in any doubt that fishing is the single greatest human-induced cause of mortality in cetaceans.

Drift-netting is one of the worst culprits and, indeed, is probably the most indiscriminate method of fishing ever devised. Hanging in the water, unseen and undetectable, drift nets are carried freely with the ocean currents and winds. Dubbed 'walls of death', or 'curtains of death', they can be hundreds of kilometres long and catch everything in their path from seabirds and turtles to whales and dolphins. In the late 1980s, for instance, the Japanese high-seas squid drift-net fisheries in the north Pacific were killing approximately 15,000–30,000 northern rightwhale dolphins, 11,000 Pacific white-sided dolphins and 6,000 Dall's porpoises every year. The United Nations took action by calling on all member nations to agree to a moratorium on drift-netting by the end of 1992. The global ban has had a very positive impact, but it is being ignored by some Asian countries and whales, dolphins and porpoises continue to be killed in large numbers by drift nets deployed inside the 200 nautical mile limit of many coastal states. More recently, the European Union banned drift-netting in almost all its waters, so progress is being made – albeit too slowly.

Gill nets are similar to drift nets in design, although much smaller, and pose another serious threat. Since they are relatively inexpensive, these death-traps are used along coastlines and in major rivers worldwide, from New Zealand and Sri Lanka to Canada and Britain. Tens of thousands of small cetaceans are believed to drown in them every year.

But perhaps the most infamous culprit, responsible for killing more dolphins in the past 35 years than any other human activity, is the tuna-fishing industry. In the eastern tropical Pacific, a stretch of ocean extending from southern California to Chile and covering an area roughly the size of Canada, it has directly caused the deaths of an estimated six to 12 million dolphins. In the worst period, during the 1960s and early 1970s, as many as half a million dolphins were being killed in the region every year. The eastern spinner dolphin stock was reduced to 44 per cent of its original size in just a few years. Fortunately, public outrage has forced the authorities to introduce new rules and regulations, which include releasing dolphins from the nets when they are captured, and the scale of the slaughter has dropped to thousands (rather than hundreds of thousands) of deaths a year. It is still too many, though, and the effects of stress from capture are an ongoing concern. There is also mounting evidence to suggest that dolphins are being set on by tuna-fishing fleets in other parts of the world.

Unfortunately, there are no easy solutions to most conflicts with fisheries. In some cases, a simple modification of the nets or the fishery management systems can have a positive effect. Educational programmes for fishermen, and newly-developed devices which alert whales and dolphins to the presence of nets, may also work in some situations. But there is no escaping the fact that much more drastic action, such as seasonal closures of some fisheries or dramatic changes in fishing techniques, may be the only effective long-term solution.

Fish on the floor of a fish market, Male, The Maldives

Pollution

Some experts predict that pollution could become the most serious threat to whales, dolphins and porpoises in the future. It is a silent, insidious and widespread killer that is already causing severe problems around the world.

Despite all the warnings, many governments continue to pretend that the world's seas and oceans have an infinite capacity to absorb the waste products of human activities. Ever-increasing quantities of industrial waste, agricultural chemicals, radioactive discharges, untreated sewage, oil, modern plastic debris and a wide variety of other pollutants are dumped directly into the sea every day – or slowly make their way there via rivers – often with devastating effect.

We are only just beginning to learn about the precise details of the damage they cause. Some pollutants are so toxic, or present in such huge quantities, that they cause immediate death. Others are more subtle in their effects, but nonetheless may be responsible for weeks, months or even years of prolonged suffering. They gradually weaken the

Rubbish on beach in Baja California, Mexico

animals, causing hormonal imbalances, a lowering of disease resistance, cancer, and many other abnormalities and chronic health problems; they may even cause a loss of fertility.

Unfortunately, whales, dolphins, porpoises and other top predators are particularly vulnerable to pollution. This is because the toxins are passed along the food chain: minute quantities are picked up by marine plankton, which are then eaten by fish and squid, and these in turn are eaten by the predators themselves. The further along the chain, the higher the concentration of toxins. Worse still, much of this build-up is passed on from one generation to another: a lactating female, through her milk, can deliver the toxins in highly concentrated doses to her young calf.

Habitat degradation, disturbance and noise pollution

One of the greatest threats to wildlife on land is habitat degradation, whether it be tropical rainforest destruction, desertification, wetland drainage or road building across important grasslands and heathland. Whales, dolphins and porpoises also suffer from habitat degradation and disturbance, although in different ways.

The main problem areas are rivers, areas close to the shore, and places near human activities further out to sea. Coastal and riverbank development, land reclamation, deep-sea dumping, oil, gas and mineral exploration, commercial fish farming, boat traffic, and the effects of land-based activities such as deforestation and river damming are all to blame. Their consequences can be quite subtle, such as increased amounts of sediment or changes in salinity, but they can also be extremely dramatic. Habitat degradation along the coast, for example, can have a far-reaching impact on the marine environment as a whole, since this is where nurseries for all kinds of invertebrates and fish form the foundation of the sea's complex food webs.

River dolphins are probably the hardest-hit by habitat degradation. The threats their habitats face include heavy boat traffic, riverbank development and dam construction.

In the case of the highly endangered Yangtze river dolphin, or baiji, for example, the world's largest hydro-electric project at the famous Three Gorges, in Hubei Province, China is likely to be the final nail in its coffin.

To make matters worse, many of the species and populations most affected by habitat degradation already have restricted distributions, or their requirements tie them to coasts or rivers and prevent them from 'escaping' to safer areas. These include all the river dolphins, the vaquita, Burmeister's porpoise, Hector's dolphin, and several large whales that move inshore at certain times of the year to breed.

Even whale watching can be a threat, if it is unregulated. Short-finned pilot whales living off the coast of Tenerife, in the Canary Islands, for example, face a veritable onslaught of whale-watch boats almost every day of the year. Many of the skippers are untrained and unconcerned about their impact on the whales, and their cavalier attitude could affect the long-term survival of the population.

One solution to the problem of habitat degradation and disturbance is to provide the animals with special sanctuaries, or marine reserves, in which they can feed and breed in relative safety. Some already exist, such as around Antarctica and in the Indian Ocean, but they need better legislation to be truly effective. And, of course, many more are needed.

But even marine sanctuaries cannot protect cetaceans from underwater noise pollution. Caused by a variety of human activities, from coastal development and seismic testing to speed boats and heavy shipping, this is a particular problem for whales, dolphins and porpoises which rely on sound for many of their day-to-day activities. Unfortunately, it is not only the loudness of a noise that is important, but its frequency as well – some frequencies are likely to be more disturbing than others, depending on the hearing range of different species. Noise may displace the animals from their feeding or breeding areas and can disrupt critical behaviours such as feeding or caring for young calves. Extremely loud noise can even kill them.

The US Navy's LFAS (Low Frequency Active Sonar) has been in the news a great deal recently – and deservedly so.

Other nations (including the UK) are already operating or planning to operate similar systems within the next few years. LFAS relies on extremely loud, low-frequency sound to detect submarines at great distances and, according to the US Navy's own studies, generates sounds of up to 140 decibels more than 500 kilometres away from the sonar source. During testing off the California coast, the noise was detected on the other side of the North Pacific.

There is growing evidence that this system is extremely harmful to cetaceans – with several mass strandings in different parts of the world coinciding with the testing of military sonar. In September 2002, for example, a mass stranding of three species of beaked whales (totalling 15 animals) occurred during European naval excercises off the Canary Islands. Research has identified a condition in at least some of the animals that resembles decompression sickness (the 'bends'), which occurs in divers who surface too quickly. It is possible that exposure to loud noise caused the whales to ascend faster than their physiology is adapted to allow. The only good news is that, following a legal ruling in 2003, peacetime use of LFAS by the US military has now been significantly limited.

Copacabana Beach, Brazil

HOW TO WATCH WHALES, DOLPHINS AND PORPOISES

Responsible whale-watching

It is sometimes easy to forget that we are uninvited guests in the world of whales, dolphins and porpoises. We are privileged to see them, but do not have a divine right. In fact, we have a responsibility to cause as little disturbance as possible – which is why whale watching should be an eyes-on, hands-off activity.

Fortunately, most whale-watch operators care about the whales, and their guests, and do a good job. They abide by local regulations or codes of conduct and put the welfare of the animals before everything else, taking care not to disturb or injure them by manoeuvring their boats carefully, slowly, and not too close, and then leaving before the whales show

Friendly grey whale,
San Ignacio
Lagoon, Mexico

signs of distress. A few operators, however, are not so careful and cause a great deal of unnecessary stress. Not only are the animals forced to steer clear of boats, or possibly even to abandon their preferred feeding or breeding grounds altogether, but collisions and other accidents can cause serious injury and even death.

The best trips also have knowledgeable naturalists on board to keep everyone well-informed; they provide free places for biologists to do urgently needed research, and they help to raise money for whale conservation. They even play a valuable role in the local economy because, with a little planning and coordination, museums, science centres, bookshops, gift shops, bus companies, hotels and guesthouses, restaurants and cafés, taxi companies and many other businesses can all benefit from the tremendous influx of visitors coming to see the whales.

In this way, the best operators put something back for the whales. Educational trips help to drum up public support for their cause; the biologists learn more about their lives and needs; there is more money available to tackle important conservation issues; and the local people have good reason to look after the whales and their marine environment.

But ultimately, of course, it is the responsibility of individual whale-watchers to choose the best and most responsible operators before booking a trip.

Clothing and equipment

The ideal choice of clothing and equipment obviously depends on where, when and how you intend to watch whales. But here are a few suggestions:

Suntan lotion and sun hat are essential to avoid sunburn and sunstroke, especially around midday. Because you are more likely to burn at sea than you are on land, use a high factor lotion.

Seasickness tablets or patches should be taken or applied in plenty of time before the trip, if you have any doubts about suffering from seasickness.

Polaroid sunglasses help to reduce the sun's glare and are excellent for seeing through reflections on the surface of the water. Remember to attach them to a safety cord.

Waterproof bags are essential for protecting your spare clothing, binoculars, cameras and other equipment from salty air and spray.

Waterproof jacket and trousers are important if sea conditions are likely to be rough or if you are expecting rain. Spending a day, or even half a day, soaked through to the skin can ruin an entire trip.

Warm and windproof clothing is vital if you are whale watching in cold weather. Remember that it is much colder at sea than it is on shore – so be careful not to underestimate how many layers you are likely to need.

Rubber-soled deck shoes are important in case the deck gets wet with spray. It is easy to slip over if you are wearing inappropriate shoes.

Field notebook and pen are invaluable (some people prefer a pocket-sized dictaphone instead). It's a good idea to copy your notes into a neat version later.

Identification guides are useful for identifying the whales, dolphins or porpoises you encounter. Consider taking guides to the birds, seals, fish and other local wildlife as well.

Binoculars are invaluable for finding whales, dolphins and porpoises, as well as for identifying them and studying their behaviour. Choose image-stabilised binoculars, or a normal pair with a magnification of 7–10x (anything higher will be unusable while you are bouncing around on a boat at sea).

Watching southern right whales, Western Cape, South Africa

A telescope (with tripod) can be useful when whale-watching from shore, or from the relatively stable platform of a large cruise ship, but the high magnification makes it virtually unusable on smaller boats.

A camera with an 80–200mm lens (or a similar zoom) is ideal but, alternatively, a fixed lens of at least 135mm can be useful for recording close encounters and interesting behaviour patterns. A motordrive is also useful. Do not forget to take plenty of film (at least twice as much as you think you will need) or, if you are using digital, plenty of card space. Use a medium to fast speed (100–200 ISO) depending on the weather and sea conditions.

Hydrophone (underwater microphone). Few whale-watchers carry hydrophones because they are quite expensive and can be difficult to use. But they do help to find some whales by sound, as well as adding a new and exciting dimension to the whale watching experience.

Safety equipment should be provided on all organised whale-watching trips. This might include life jackets, life rafts, flares, a VHF radio, and first aid equipment.

Whale crier,
South Africa

Finding the animals at sea

In theory, it is possible to see whales, dolphins and porpoises almost anywhere in the world. They are found near the poles, at the equator, in freshwater rivers, along shallow coastlines, and even in the deep waters of the open sea.

But many species tend to be plentiful only in particular areas and, even then, are present only at certain times of the year. Their distribution also varies weekly, daily and hourly, according to many different factors such as sea and weather conditions, food availability and human disturbance. To add to the challenge, they can be very difficult to spot in anything but the calmest conditions – even if you are very close to them.

People with a lot of experience at sea instinctively recognise the tiniest clues when they are looking for cetaceans. They are trained to register the slightest movements and splashes that give their presence away. With a large whale, for example, the first clue is often its blow or spout. This is more visible in some weather conditions than others, but it can be surprisingly distinctive. It may look like a flash of white (especially against a dark background) or a more gradual puff of smoke. Blows are easy to miss, though, especially since there is often a considerable gap between each one.

Challenging conditions on the Drake Passage

Alternatively, you may briefly see the head and back of the whale break the surface. This often resembles a strange wave that, somehow, does not look quite right. Anything suspicious, even if nine times out of 10 it does turn out to be a wave, is worth investigating. Splashes are also good clues. They can be caused by a large whale breaching, flipper-slapping or lobtailing – or by dolphins. A group of dolphins in the distance frequently looks like a rough patch of water, resembling lots of whitecaps and little breaking waves. The presence of birds can often be a tell-tale sign as well, particularly if they seem to be feeding or are concentrated in one particular area. It makes sense that, if they have found a school of fish, there could be whales or dolphins feeding underneath.

Finally, do not forget to look *everywhere* – in front, behind, and to both sides. Scan the horizon with binoculars and use the naked eye to check nearer the boat (it is amazing how often people miss dolphins bow-riding right in front of them because they are too busy looking far out to sea). The golden rule is to be patient because, even in areas with well-known cetacean populations, it may take a while to track them down.

Problems of identification

Identifying whales, dolphins and porpoises at sea is a real challenge. In fact, it can be so difficult that even the world's experts are unable to identify every species they encounter: on most official surveys, at least some sightings have to be logged as 'unidentified'. But despite the inevitable frustrations, developing the necessary skills to tell one species from another can also be very satisfying.

There are a number of different problems to overcome. The first, quite simply, is being on a boat: making detailed observations while trying to keep balance on a rolling, slippery deck can be difficult at the best of times. Adverse sea and weather conditions, such as a heavy swell, whitecaps, high winds, driving rain, or even glaring sunshine, add to the difficulties by making it almost impossible to get a good view and an accurate impression of the main features of the animal.

Then there are the whales, dolphins and porpoises themselves. They spend most of their lives underwater and, even when they come to the surface to breathe, frequently reveal little more than a brief glimpse of their dorsal fins and backs. Even a good view can be confusing, since many species look alike: it takes a highly trained eye to tell the difference between a pygmy sperm whale and a dwarf sperm whale, for example.

At the same time, individuals of the same species frequently vary so much that they are rarely identical. Their dorsal fins are shaped differently, they show variations in their colouring, behave differently, and even come in a range of different sizes. Adult bottlenose dolphins, for example, vary in size from just under two metres to nearly four metres.

However, despite all these potential pitfalls, it is quite possible for anyone to recognise the relatively common and distinctive species and, eventually, many of the more unusual ones as well. It just requires some background knowledge and a little practice.

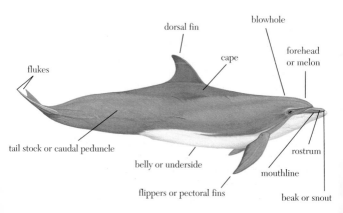

blowhole

dorsal fin

cape

forehead or melon

flukes

tail stock or caudal peduncle

belly or underside

rostrum

mouthline

flippers or pectoral fins

beak or snout

Identification checklist

The easiest way to identify whales, dolphins and porpoises is to use a relatively simple process of elimination. This involves running through a mental checklist of 14 key features every time a new animal is encountered at sea. It is not often possible to use all 14 features, and one alone is rarely enough for a positive identification, but the best approach is to gather information on as many as possible before drawing any firm conclusions.

Geographical location: There is not a single place in the world where all 84 cetacean species have been recorded. In fact, there are not many places with records of more than a few dozen species. This immediately helps to cut down on the number of possibilities. Atlantic white-sided dolphins, for example, occur only in the north Atlantic, while Pacific white-sided dolphins occur only in the north Pacific.

Habitat: Just as cheetahs live on open plains rather than in jungles, and snow leopards prefer mountains to wetlands, most whales, dolphins and porpoises are adapted to specific marine or freshwater habitats. For example, Hector's dolphins are unlikely to be encountered far out to sea, while sperm whales are unlikely to be seen in shallow water.

Killer whale, northern Norway

Size: It is difficult to estimate size accurately at sea, unless a direct comparison can be made with the length of the boat or another object in the water. Therefore it is better to use three simple categories: up to three metres, three to 10 metres, and over 10 metres. In this way, simply by deciding whether the animal is small, medium or large helps to eliminate a wide range of possibilities.

Unusual features: Some cetaceans have very unusual features, which can be used for a quick identification. These include the extraordinary long tusk of the male narwhal and the callosities covering the heads of right whales.

Dorsal fin: The size, shape and position of the dorsal fin varies greatly between species. Some fins are tall and triangular, others are rounded, a few are little more than a hump, some have broad bases, others have narrow bases, some are curved, others are upright, and there is every possible combination in between; and, of course, a few species have no dorsal fin at all. The position of the fin on the animal's back – in the middle, towards the head or towards the tail – is also a useful identification feature.

Flippers: The length, colour and shape of the flippers, as well as their position on the animal's body, vary greatly from

Bryde's whale, Shikoku Island, Japan

Spinner dolphin, The Maldives

one species to another. It is not always possible to see them, but flippers can be useful for identification in some species: in the humpback whale, for example, they are unmistakable.

Body shape: Much of the time, whales, dolphins and porpoises do not show enough of themselves to provide an overall impression of their shape. Sometimes, however, this can be a useful feature. For example, the vaquita has a noticeably robust body shape, while the finless porpoise is quite slender and streamlined.

Beak: The presence or absence of a prominent beak is a particularly useful identification feature in toothed whales. The Irrawaddy dolphin, for instance, has a rounded head without an obvious beak, whereas the spinner dolphin has a very long, narrow beak.

Colour and markings: Many cetaceans are surprisingly colourful, and have distinctive markings such as body stripes or eye patches. Commerson's dolphins, for example, are markedly black and white, while Risso's dolphins are usually covered in white scratches and scars. Unfortunately, more subtle markings can be difficult to use for identification purposes, because colours at sea vary according to water clarity and light conditions. Also, bear in mind that the animal can appear much darker than normal if it is viewed against the sun.

Flukes: The flukes can be important features for identifying larger whales: some species lift their flukes high into the air before they dive, others do not. Minke and sei whales generally do not, for example, while humpbacks and sperm whales frequently do. It is also worth checking the shape of the flukes, looking for any distinctive markings and noticing whether or not there is a notch between the trailing edges.

Blow or spout: The blow is only really visible in larger whales. But it varies in height, shape and visibility between species and, especially on calm days, can be extremely useful for identification purposes. Although variations in the blow between individuals can make it a tricky means of identification, experienced observers can tell one species from another even from a considerable distance. Right whales, for example, have wide, V-shaped blows, whereas fin whales produce single, narrow columns of spray.

Dive sequence: The dive sequence can be suprisingly distinctive in many species. Variations include: the angle at which the head breaks the surface; whether or not the dorsal fin and blowhole are visible at the same time; how strongly the tail stock is arched; the time interval between breaths; and the number of breaths before a deep dive.

Behaviour: Some species are more active at the surface than others, so any unusual behaviour can sometimes be useful for identification purposes. Among the large whales, for instance, humpbacks and right whales breach much more often than fin whales and blue whales.

Group size: Since some species are highly gregarious, while others tend to live alone or in small groups, it is worth noting the number of animals seen together. Fin whales, for example, are normally seen alone or in small groups, whereas there could be dozens or hundreds of long-finned pilot whales travelling together, or literally thousands of common dolphins.

Short-finned pilot whales, Sea of Cortez, Mexico

The golden rule

It is often tempting to guess the identification of an unusual whale, dolphin or porpoise that you have not seen very clearly. But this is a mistake. Apart from the fact that it is bad science, it does little to improve your identification skills. Working hard at identification – and then enjoying the satisfaction of knowing that an animal has been identified correctly – is what makes a real expert in the long term.

It is perfectly acceptable to record simply 'unidentified dolphin' or 'unidentified whale', if a more accurate identification is not possible. But do write detailed notes for reference at a later date. As well as helping to improve your field skills, these notes may enable repeat sightings of species previously recorded as 'unidentified' to be turned into a positive identification days, weeks, months or even years later.

Recognising behaviour patterns

Whales, dolphins and porpoises are active animals and some of their more impressive and energetic displays take place in full view on the surface of the water. They slap the water with their flippers, fins or tails, ride in the bow waves and wakes of boats, lift their heads above the surface, and even leap high into the air and land back in the water with a tremendous splash.

Grey whale, San Ignacio Lagoon, Mexico

We do not fully understand the meaning of many of these displays and, of course, it is quite possible that there are different explanations for different occasions, according to the species, the age and sex of the animal, and the context in which the activities are taking place.

However, a great deal of behavioural research has been done in recent years and, at last, we are beginning to unravel some of their secrets. Slapping the surface, for example, may be a form of courtship display, a way of signalling across great distances underwater, a technique for herding fish or dislodging parasites, a show of strength or a challenge... or, in some cases, it could simply be for fun.

Breaching: When a whale launches itself into the air head-first, and falls back into the water with a splash, it is said to be breaching. Most species have been observed breaching at one time or another, although some do it more often than others. Tail breaching is similar, but is tail-first instead of head-first and rarely lifts the whale as far out of the water.

Flipper-slapping: Many cetaceans lie on their sides or backs and slap one or both of their flippers onto the surface with a resounding splash. This is known as flipper-slapping, pectoral-slapping, pec-slapping or flipper-flopping.

Lobtailing: Lobtailing is an impressive display, especially in large whales, involving the forceful slapping of the flukes against the surface of the water. Also known as tail-slapping, it is done while the main body of the whale lies just under the surface.

Southern right whale, Western Cape, South Africa

Blowing or spouting: The blow or spout is the cloud of condensed air and atomised water droplets (not water) produced above a whale's head when it breathes out. It is also the term used to describe the actual act of breathing. In most small whales, dolphins and porpoises, the blow is low, brief and barely visible, but in large whales it can be very distinctive.

Fluking: When some large whales make a deep dive from the surface, they lift their tails high into the air to thrust their bodies into a more steeply-angled descent toward deeper waters. Bowheads, right whales, greys, blues, humpbacks and sperm whales all lift their flukes regularly, while a number of other species do from time to time. All whales leave a 'flukeprint' at the surface – a circular swirl looking like a patch of oil – made by turbulence from the movement of the flukes.

Spyhopping: Spyhopping is the term used to describe an interesting form of behaviour in which whales and dolphins poke their heads above the surface of the water, apparently to have a look around. Most species can see both above and below the surface.

Wake-riding: Swimming in the frothy wake of a boat or ship seems to be a favourite pastime of many dolphins, as well as some whales and porpoises. They surf, twist and turn in the waves, and even splash around and swim upside-down in the bubbles.

Logging: It is not uncommon to see groups of whales floating motionless at the surface together, usually all facing in the same direction. Known as logging, this is a form of rest.

Porpoising: When travelling at speed, many cetaceans literally leave the water each time they take a breath. Also known as running, this is believed to reduce friction on their bodies when they break the surface, which may help to conserve energy.

Bow-riding: Many dolphins, and some whales and porpoises, ride the bow-waves of boats and ships, jostling for the best position where they can be pushed along in the water by the force of the wave. Certain dolphins even ride the bow-waves of large whales in exactly the same way. On some occasions they may simply be hitching a free ride but, when they actively go out of their way to ride in the bow-waves, it is difficult to imagine that it can be anything more than exuberant play.

Bow-riding Heaviside's dolphins, Western Cape, South Africa

HOW WHALES AND DOLPHINS ARE STUDIED

Research on wild whales is staggeringly new. It is so new, in fact, that whale biologists have yet to monitor a single generation of large whales through one complete life cycle, from the moment they are born to their last days and ultimately to death through old age.

For years, the prospect of studying whales must have seemed about as difficult and challenging as exploring outer space. After all, these are animals that often live in extremely remote areas far out to sea, spend much of their lives diving to great depths underwater, and then show little of themselves when they rise to the surface to breathe. Many are quite shy and elusive, as well, and tend to avoid boats so, even at the surface, close encounters with them are almost impossible.

From early beginnings to high-tech research

For a long time, the only information we had came from dead animals washed ashore, or killed by fishermen, and from some of the millions of whales slaughtered by commercial whalers. Then scientists began to study captive bottlenose dolphins and other small cetaceans in their concrete tanks.

But as we accumulated a wealth of data on basic whale biology, our knowledge of their lives under natural conditions, wild and free, was severely limited. In the days when modern technology had already taken us to the Moon and beyond, we were only just beginning to understand these extraordinary forms of intelligent life on our own planet. As one biologist commented, 'the best we can say is that our knowledge of whales, dolphins and porpoises has progressed from almost nothing to just a little bit'.

The first attempts at wild whale research concentrated simply on counting whales – dead ones, initially, because they were so much easier to count than live ones. It was not until the late 1960s and early 1970s that a few pioneer biologists began the painstaking process of counting live whales, and then trying to learn more about their feeding techniques, breeding habits, migrations and other aspects of their daily lives.

Gradually, more and more people became involved in whale research, and their information-gathering techniques became increasingly sophisticated. In the past decade, the number of researchers, projects and study locations has increased exponentially, while whale research itself has become a leading branch of natural science.

Modern whale researchers still study whales in the traditional sense, simply watching them through binoculars, for example, or leaning out of boats to scoop up their faeces for examination. But, at the same time, they frequently enlist the help of state-of-the-art equipment and the kind of enterprising and visionary research techniques that would make NASA proud.

Satellites in space, deep-sea submersibles, radio transmitters, high-tech directional hydrophones, complex computer programmes, fibre optics, deepwater video

Bottlenose dolphin, Sea of Cortez, Mexico

probes, DNA fingerprinting and, most recently, the US Navy's Integrated Underwater Surveillance System are now all part of the modern whale researcher's armoury.

Photo-identification

Biologists have been identifying individual animals as part of their research for a long time. It is an invaluable way of following their movements, activities and associations over periods of days, weeks, months and even years. Jane Goodall used facial patterns to recognise all the chimpanzees in her classic study in Gombe National Park, Tanzania, for example; more recent studies have used striping patterns in zebras, the arrangement of whiskers in lions, and even the shapes, nicks and scars of elephants' ears to tell one animal from another.

Whale and dolphin biologists are no exception, and they identify individuals in many different ways. Blue whales can be recognised by the shape of the dorsal fin and the pattern of mottling on the body; individual humpback whales, on the other hand, are recognised by the unique black-and-white markings on the underside of the tail. The differences can often be quite subtle, so each animal is photographed to confirm its identity and to provide a permanent record of its existence. This technique is known as 'photo-identification', or 'photo-ID', and has dramatically extended our knowledge of wild cetaceans in recent years.

DNA fingerprinting

Do different calves with the same mother share the same father? Are individuals that spend a lot of time together related? These and many other intriguing questions can be answered just by examining a small piece of a whale's skin. More accurately, it is the genetic material, or DNA, in the skin that is so revealing. Just as one person's fingerprints are different from everyone else's, no two animals have exactly the same DNA – yet related animals show some similarities. The clever detective work involved in interpreting this information is called 'DNA fingerprinting', and it has proved invaluable in wild whale research.

Radio- and satellite-telemetry

It is possible to attach a specially
designed transmitter to a whale or
dolphin and then follow its
movements from a boat, a light
aircraft or even a research
laboratory on the other side
of the world. Some
transmitters are merely
tracking devices, but
more sophisticated
models can also
provide
information on
the animal's swimming patterns, dive depths and heart rate,
as well as environmental conditions, water temperature, and
much more. There are basically two kinds of transmitter:
radio transmitters, which send signals directly to receivers
nearby, and satellite transmitters, which beam the signals up
to orbiting communications satellites and from there back to
receiving stations anywhere on Earth.

Eavesdropping on the underwater world

Whales, dolphins and porpoises live in a world that is
dominated by sound, and a great deal can be learnt by listening
to them underwater. This is such a challenging area of research
that it has been likened to trying to find out what goes on in
New York by dangling a microphone from the top of the
Empire State Building. But experienced whale scientists using
sophisticated underwater microphones, called hydrophones,
have been making some exciting discoveries in recent years.

A major development in this field came in 1992, when the
US Navy opened its doors to the so-called Integrated
Underwater Surveillance System. A series of sophisticated
underwater listening stations on the seabed, originally designed
for tracking enemy submarines, this offers some tremendously
exciting possibilities for whale research in the future.

73

The whale jigsaw

There are still no short-cuts in whale research but, in recent years, the growth in our knowledge has been nothing short of remarkable. Studying such elusive creatures is all about being content with tiny snippets of information that must be assembled into a coherent picture over periods of many years. It is like piecing together an enormously complicated jigsaw puzzle, where each piece brings with it new questions and unexpected surprises. The main difference, of course, is that the whale jigsaw will never be completely finished. Nevertheless, it is encouraging to know that we have probably added more pieces in the past 10 or 20 years than ever before.

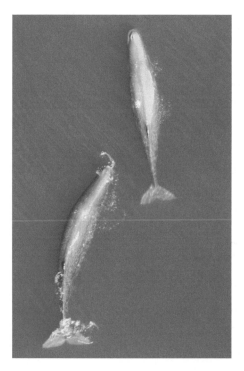

Sperm whales, Sea of Cortez, Mexico

Grey Whale
Eschrichtius robustus

ID FACT FILE

OTHER NAMES
California grey
whale, mussel-
digger, devilfish,
scrag whale.

MAXIMUM LENGTH
15 metres.

MAXIMUM WEIGHT
35 tonnes.

FIELD ID
Mottled grey; low
hump instead of
fin; 'knuckles'
between hump
and tail; low
heart-shaped
blow; narrow
head with
barnacles and
whale lice;
usually raises
flukes when
diving.

DIET
Mainly benthic
amphipods,
filtered from
bottom
sediment; also
midwater fish
and crustaceans.

BREEDING
Calves every 2–3
years; gestation
12–13 months.

By the time the grey whale was being given official protection, in the late 1930s, it was already extinct in the North Atlantic and was dangerously close to extinction in the North Pacific. It is unclear why the North Atlantic population had disappeared a few hundred years earlier, but whaling in the North Pacific was so intense that it left no more than a few hundred survivors. Fortunately, there were just enough for the grey whale to make a remarkable comeback – so remarkable, in fact, that its recovery is unmatched by any other species of great whale. The current population of some 26,000 Californian grey whales may even exceed pre-exploitation levels. However, the population in the western North Pacific is still critically endangered, with as few as 100 animals remaining. Once dubbed the devilfish by whalers, for their ferocity in the face of danger, grey whales are better known these days for their friendly behaviour and curious approaches to boats.

Where to look
Grey whales are found only in the North Pacific. The eastern population (Californian stock) migrates on average about 8,000 kilometres

GREY WHALE

between its summer feeding grounds in the
Arctic's Bering, Chukchi and western Beaufort
seas and its winter breeding grounds around Baja
California, Mexico. The western population
(Korean stock) spends the summer in the Sea of
Okhotsk and is believed to breed in tropical waters
off southern China.

INCREDIBLE JOURNEYS OF THE GREY WHALE

Grey whales are inveterate travellers, commuting along the entire length of the North American coastline, and back again, every year. The round-trip distance between their winter breeding grounds in Baja California, Mexico, and their summer feeding grounds in the Bering Sea can be as much as 20,000 kilometres, making their journey one of the longest migrations of any mammal. The migration north tends to be close to shore and in good weather, the one south often takes place in stormier weather and is usually a little further offshore (although still within sight of land).

Feeding in the Arctic: April–October

The vast majority of grey whales spend every summer in the Bering, Chukchi and western Beaufort seas where, for about five months of the year, they eat as much as they possibly can. Feeding in relatively shallow water, they use their mouths like vacuum cleaners and literally suck up sediment from the seabed. They sieve this with their baleen plates, and then swallow the tiny crustaceans trapped inside. Each adult grey whale eats nearly 70 tonnes of these little creatures in one summer-long feast. Their aim is to put on enough body weight, in the form of blubber and fat, to survive the rest of the year without food.

Migrating south: November–February

Early in October, the Arctic weather begins to worsen and the whales prepare themselves to leave. Their migration south is organised like a military manoeuvre: the pregnant females are first to go, followed by non-pregnant females, then mature males, immature females next and, finally, the immature males. Over a period of several months, they file through Unimak Pass, a narrow gap between islands in the Aleutian chain, and head south. By the second week of January, huge numbers are passing southern California. With hardly a break, they average about 125 kilometres a day, and the entire journey takes them a couple of months.

Breeding in the sub-tropics: December–April

The pregnant females are the first to arrive in the breeding
lagoons along the Pacific coast of Baja California, Mexico.
They give birth to their calves, in the shallow backwaters,
while many of the other whales are still on their way south.
The calves drink huge quantities of their mothers' fat-laden
milk and gain weight rapidly. It is a race against time, because
within a few months they will have to be fit and ready for
their first journey north.

Migrating north: February–June

The grey whales tend to swim a little slower on their journey
north (perhaps 70–90 kilometres a day) and the females with
calves, especially, rest for a few hours or even a few days at a
time. Funnelling back into the Bering Sea, through Unimak
Pass, they fan out across their Arctic feeding grounds for
another summer. It will only be a few months before they are
ready to leave once again and, as one yearly cycle comes to an
end, another begins.

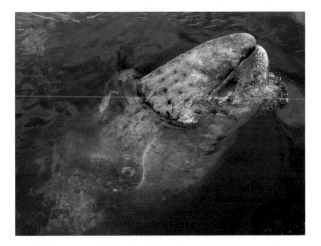

Southern Right Whale
Eubalaena australis

With their enormous heads covered in strange-looking callosities (hardened patches of skin), their dark, rotund bodies, and their lack of a dorsal fin, northern and southern right whales look almost identical. But they have long been considered distinct species and this separation has recently been supported by genetic evidence. Southern right whales have been studied since 1970 – longer than any other baleen whale – when Roger Payne began to recognise individuals by the shape and pattern of their callosities at Peninsula Valdés, Argentina. Right whales are particularly active at the surface and can often be seen breaching, lobtailing, spyhopping and even sailing (they raise flukes in the air and then sail downwind before swimming back to the starting point for another go). Their mating system is unusual among whales because it is heavily dependent on sperm competition (male right whales have the largest testes in the animal kingdom – weighing nearly a tonne) rather than competition between individuals.

Where to look

The southern right whale has a circumpolar distribution in the southern hemisphere. It breeds in South America, southern Africa and Australasia (and off several remote offshore islands such as Crozet and Kerguelen). Its summer feeding grounds are in colder waters around Antarctica and elsewhere in the Southern Ocean. Exploited heavily during the nineteenth century, its numbers now appear to be recovering well.

Northern Right Whale

Eubalaena glacialis (North Atlantic)

Eubalaena japonica (North Pacific)

ID FACT FILE

OTHER NAMES
Black right whale, Biscayan right whale, Nordkaper.

MAXIMUM LENGTH
18 metres.

MAXIMUM WEIGHT
100 tonnes.

FIELD ID
Black with irregular white patches on underside; broad back with no fin; large head covered in callosities; strongly arched mouthline; large paddle-shaped flippers; V-shaped blow; usually raises flukes when diving.

DIET
Mainly copepods (which are so small about 8,000 would fit in a teaspoon); occasionally krill.

BREEDING
Calves every 3–5 years; gestation 12 months.

Recent genetic evidence suggests that there are two species of northern right whale, and that they have been evolving separately for millennia. However, they look virtually identical with their raised and roughened patches of skin, known as callosities. These occur on the whales in approximately the same places as facial hair on human males and, although they are black, usually appear white or orangey-white due to massive infestations of whale lice. Callosities are found on both sexes and young calves, but their purpose is unknown. Northern right whales are the rarest large whales in the world and have never recovered from years of heavy exploitation by whalers. There are only about 300 North Atlantic right whales surviving today. Estimates for North Pacific right whales are less precise, but there are probably fewer than 100 left in the eastern population (just one calf has been seen here in the past century) and possibly a few hundred in the western population.

Where to look

The largest population is in the western North
Atlantic – mainly off Cape Cod in spring, the Bay of
Fundy and the Scotia Shelf in summer, and on
breeding grounds off Florida and Georgia in winter.
There are very occasional sightings in European
waters. Small numbers survive in the North Pacific,
mainly from the Sea of Okhotsk east to the Gulf of
Alaska, with occasional sightings off the United
States and Baja California, Mexico.

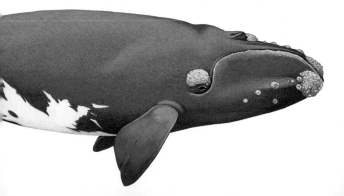

NORTHERN RIGHT WHALES: ON THE VERGE OF EXTINCTION

North Atlantic right whales were probably the first whales to be hunted commercially: Basque whalers were killing them in the Bay of Biscay, north of Spain, as early as the eleventh century. The whales were killed primarily for their oil, which was distributed throughout Europe, but the Basques found a market for almost every part of their catch and even the excrement was used (for dyeing fabrics red). The whaling had spread to eastern Canada by 1530 and to New England by the 1600s and right whales continued to be popular targets for commercial whalers for many centuries. Whaling of North Pacific right whales began considerably later, in the Gulf of Alaska in 1835, but was no less intensive.

Named for being the 'right' whales to catch, they were easy to approach, slow swimmers, lived close to shore, normally floated when dead, and provided large quantities of valuable oil, meat and baleen (whalebone). By the early 1900s, tens or even hundreds of thousands of them had been killed, and all three species were critically close to extinction.

All right whale populations worldwide were protected from commercial whaling in the late 1930s, although some were killed illegally by Japan, Brazil and the Soviet Union well into the 1950s and 1960s. But even after decades of international legal protection, only the southern right whale is showing signs of recovery.

Although the whaling has ceased, North Atlantic right whales are now threatened by heavy shipping and entanglement in commercial fishing gear. Between 1970 and 1999, no fewer than 16 were known to have been killed in collisions with ships (and two others probably died of their injuries), while three are known to have drowned in fishing nets and a further eight were seriously injured and probably died too. When the surviving population is so small, these are significant numbers. The sad fact is that northern right whales are among the world's most critically endangered mammals and are probably closer to extinction than any other large whale.

Pygmy Right Whale
Caperea marginata

ID FACT FILE

OTHER NAMES
None.
MAXIMUM LENGTH
6.5 metres.
MAXIMUM WEIGHT
3.4 tonnes.
FIELD ID
Quite small and sleek; grey upperside, paler underside; pronounced falcate fin; may be twin chevrons on back and sides; strongly arched mouthline; no callosities on head; indistinct blow; undemonstrative behaviour; rarely raises flukes when diving.
DIET
Probably copepods, but also some krill.
BREEDING
Calving interval and gestation period unknown.

The pygmy right whale is the smallest species of baleen whale and one of the least-known cetaceans. Our knowledge is based on fewer than 20 sightings at sea and a few dozen dead animals caught by fishermen or washed ashore. Like the other right whales it has a strongly arched lower jaw, but it differs from them in having a pronounced dorsal fin and no callosities. It is the only baleen whale that has not been the target of large-scale commercial whaling and the only known threat is occasional drownings in fishing nets off South Africa. Pygmy right whales are usually seen alone or in pairs, although large aggregations of as many as 80 individuals have been recorded. Virtually nothing is known about their social structure or behaviour. Unless it is possible to see the distinctive arched mouthline, they can be very difficult to distinguish from dwarf and Antarctic minke whales at sea.

Where to look
The pygmy right whale is known from a small number of widely dispersed records across temperate waters of the southern hemisphere (never south of the Antarctic Convergence). It has been recorded mainly in Australasia, South Africa, South America and a few islands in between.

Bowhead Whale

Balaena mysticetus

ID FACT FILE

OTHER NAMES
Greenland right
whale, Greenland
whale, Arctic
right whale,
Arctic whale.

MAXIMUM LENGTH
20 metres.

MAXIMUM WEIGHT
90 tonnes.

FIELD ID
Black, rotund
body; no fin;
irregular white
patch on chin
with black spots;
two distinct
humps in profile;
huge head;
strongly arched
mouth; V-shaped
blow; no
callosities or
barnacles; often
raises flukes
when diving.

DIET
Mainly krill and
copepods, but
also other
invertebrates.

BREEDING
Calves every 3–4
years; gestation
probably 13–14
months.

The only large whale found exclusively in the Arctic, the bowhead is well adapted to life in its freezing home. With a layer of blubber up to 50 centimetres thick, and an ability to create its own breathing holes by breaking through ice up to 1.8 metres thick, it is able to live in higher latitudes than any other baleen whale. Its distinctive head is almost triangular in profile and, when lying at the surface, forms the first of two humps (the second is the back) that make it resemble the shape of the Loch Ness Monster. There is growing evidence that, like humpback whales, bowhead males produce songs that may advertise for females. Heavily hunted by commercial whalers for several centuries, and still being taken by small-scale indigenous whalers, the bowhead is not particularly common. The total number of survivors is estimated to be only 8,000–9,000, and most of these

live in a single population in the Bering, Chukchi
and Beaufort Seas. The remaining four recognised
populations are highly endangered.

Where to look
Bowhead whales are found in cold waters around
the Arctic and sub-Arctic, rarely far from the pack
ice. They normally migrate to the high Arctic in
spring and summer, as the sea ice breaks up and
recedes, and then retreat southwards with the
advancing ice edge in autumn and winter.

Humpback Whale

Megaptera novaeangliae

ID FACT FILE

OTHER NAMES
Hump-backed whale.
MAXIMUM LENGTH
17 metres.
MAXIMUM WEIGHT
40 tonnes.
FIELD ID
Stocky body; black upperside, white, black or mottled underside; low, stubby fin often on a hump; extremely long flippers white below and white or black (North Pacific) above; single, bushy blow; variable black-and-white fluke pattern; often raises flukes when diving.

DIET
Krill and variety of small schooling fish.
BREEDING
Calves every 2–3 years; gestation about 12 months.

The humpback whale is relatively well studied, yet many aspects of its life are still shrouded in mystery and we are only just beginning to unravel some of its best-kept secrets. It is renowned for its long flippers, which can grow to nearly a third of its body length and give the humpback its scientific name (*Megaptera novaeangliae* means 'big-winged New Englander' – New England being where the first specimen was described). Its head is also distinctive, with a series of knobs or tubercles covering the rostrum and much of the lower jaw; about the size of a golf ball, each knob is a hair follicle with a single, coarse hair growing out of its centre. Humpbacks are among the most energetic of all the large whales and are well known for their spectacular breaching, as well as lobtailing, flipper-

slapping and spyhopping. Even when they seem to be resting, they are fun to watch and may lie on their backs, or sides, holding their enormous flippers high in the air.

Where to look
Widely distributed from the poles to the tropics, humpbacks feed in cool waters during spring and summer and breed in warmer water during the winter. They migrate farther than most other cetaceans – making a round-trip journey of up to 16,000 kilometres. Nearly a quarter of a million were killed by commercial whalers, but they seem to be making a good recovery in many parts of their range.

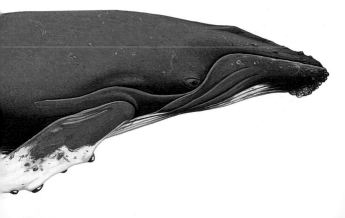

FISHING WITH NETS OF BUBBLES

Humpback whales have developed an extraordinarily diverse and ingenious range of techniques for catching their food. They lunge through patches of fish or krill with their mouths wide open, literally gulping vast mouthfuls out of the ocean, and even stun their prey with slaps of their flippers or flukes.

But no fishing technique is more impressive than fishing with bubbles. Many humpbacks use huge, explosive bubble clouds, releasing a single blast up to 20 metres across that probably concentrates and disorientates their prey. But to catch herring in the northern North Pacific and Bering Sea they prefer more delicate bubble nets, which strongly resemble man-made seine nets both in design and in the way they are deployed.

Known simply as 'bubble-netting', this particular fishing technique is all the more sensational because the climax of the action takes place in full view above the surface of the water.

When a humpback whale forms a bubble net on its own, it dives beneath a school of fish and starts to release bubbles from its blowholes. Then it swims slowly towards the surface, in a spiral, to form a circular barrier of bubbles around the school. As soon as the 'net' is complete, it swims through the centre with its mouth wide open. The water is flushed out through the baleen plates, as the whale rises above the surface, and the fish trapped inside its mouth are swept up by the tongue and swallowed.

Incredibly, as many as 20 humpback whales may work together in a more complex form of bubble-net fishing, requiring an almost incomprehensible level of coordination.

It begins with all the members of a fishing group swimming slowly at the surface, spending a few minutes resting and catching their collective breath. Then they all dive and disappear beneath the surface together. No one knows quite how they organise themselves underwater but, after about five or 10 minutes, bubbles begin to break the surface, each one roughly the size of a dinner plate. These form part of a huge circle that can be up to 45 metres across. Suddenly, hundreds of tonnes of blubber and gaping mouths erupt from within the circle in one great foaming mass. With water gushing down their distended throat pleats, and fish leaping for their lives, the whales explode to a height of nearly six metres before sinking back into the depths. It is one of the greatest wildlife spectacles on Earth.

Opposite: Lunge-feeding humpback whale, south-east Alaska

SINGING HUMPBACKS

Drop a hydrophone into the water in an area where
humpback whales are breeding and you may hear a baffling
medley of moans, groans, roars, snores, squeaks and
whistles. These are the unearthly, hauntingly beautiful
sounds made by male humpback whales, which are famous
for singing the longest and most complex songs in the
animal kingdom.

The singing whales hang almost upside-down in the
water, often fairly close to the surface. With their eyes
closed and their heads pointing towards the seabed, they
sometimes wave their enormous flippers up and down like
conductors in front of an orchestra.

Humpback whale, Silver Bank, Dominican Republic

No one knows exactly how they sing. They have no vocal chords and, intriguingly, while they are in full song, no air is released. They do not even open their mouths. The latest theory is that they shift air around inside their bodies, but much more research is needed before it is possible to be sure of the details.

They sing throughout the day and night – and may continue for 24 hours or even longer with hardly a break. Because most of the singing takes place at the breeding grounds, and exclusively by males, it is probably used to woo females and to warn away unwanted competition from rival males. But it is also possible that the songs have more subtle meanings and nuances that we do not yet understand.

A song can last for as long as half an hour and, as soon as the whale has finished, it simply goes back to the beginning and sings the same song all over again. Each song consists of several main components, or phrases, which are always sung in the same order and are repeated a number of times but are forever being refined and improved. This means that the song heard one day is quite different to the one being heard several months later. When the whales return to their breeding grounds the following winter, they immediately start singing the version of the song that was in vogue at the end of the previous breeding season.

Even more extraordinary is the fact that all the humpbacks in one area sing broadly the same song, incorporating each other's improvisations as they go along. It is as if they compose and then re-write the 'music' together. In this way, the entire composition changes over a period of several years.

Meanwhile, humpback whales in other oceans sing very different compositions. They probably all croon about the same trials and tribulations in life, but it is as if the ones living around Hawaii sing in American English, while those living off the coast of the Dominican Republic, for example, sing in Caribbean English. The differences are so distinctive that experts can tell where a whale was recorded simply by listening to the intricacies of its own special dialect.

Common Minke Whale

Balaenoptera acutorostrata

ID FACT FILE

OTHER NAMES
Little finner, little
piked whale,
pikehead, lesser
finback, lesser
rorqual.

MAXIMUM LENGTH
10.7 metres.

MAXIMUM WEIGHT
9 tonnes.

FIELD ID
Small and sleek;
dark upperside,
white underside;
sharply-pointed
snout; snout
breaks surface
first; falcate fin;
white bands on
flippers in many
populations;
indistinct or
invisible blow;
does not raise
flukes when
diving.

DIET
Mainly small
schooling fish
and krill.

BREEDING
Calves every 1–2
years; gestation
about 10
months.

The common minke is the second smallest baleen whale, after the pygmy right, and is also the commonest. Reputedly named after a novice eighteenth-century Norwegian whaler, named Meincke, it is a frequent sight on whale-watch trips in many parts of the world. Surprisingly little is known about many aspects of its life, though, and limited evidence suggests an intriguingly complex social structure with populations segregated by age, sex or reproductive condition. Minkes are quite variable in appearance: animals in the northern hemisphere, for example, have a white band on their flippers, but this extends into a white shoulder patch or is absent on many southern hemisphere animals. Two sub-species are recognised – North Atlantic minke whale (*Balaenoptera acutorostrata acutorostrata*) and North Pacific minke whale (*Balaenoptera acutorostrata scammoni*) – and there may be a third, known as the dwarf minke whale for its smaller size, found only in the southern hemisphere. Minkes are curious and will approach boats.

Where to look
Found virtually worldwide from the tropics to the
edge of the polar ice, mainly in warmer waters in
winter and cooler waters in summer. The minke
whale's small size saved it from commercial whalers
until the twentieth century, but many tens of
thousands have been killed in the last hundred
years. It is still being hunted today, by Norway and
Iceland in the North Atlantic and Japan in the
North Pacific and the Antarctic.

Antarctic Minke Whale

Balaenoptera bonaerensis

ID FACT FILE

OTHER NAMES
Little finner, little piked whale, pikehead, lesser finback, lesser rorqual.

MAXIMUM LENGTH
10.7 metres.

MAXIMUM WEIGHT
9 tonnes.

FIELD ID
Small and sleek; dark upperside, white underside; asymmetrical baleen colouration; sharply-pointed snout; snout breaks surface first; falcate fin; flippers may be light-coloured but no white bands; indistinct or invisible blow; does not raise flukes when diving.

DIET
Mainly krill, but sometimes small schooling fish.

BREEDING
Calves every 1–2 years; gestation about 10 months.

A new species of minke whale, the Antarctic minke, was officially recognised in the late 1990s. It differs significantly from the common minke in many external and skeletal features (its baleen plates, for example, have an asymmetrical colouration) and the two species are so genetically different that they are more closely related to sei and Bryde's whales than they are to each other. However, they can be difficult to tell apart at sea. Antarctic minkes overlap in range with dwarf minkes (a smaller form of the common minke) but on average are a full two metres longer. They are usually seen alone or in small groups, although larger gatherings are sometimes encountered on good feeding grounds. They are believed to form a significant part of the diet of Antarctic killer whales and are still being killed by Japan for the dubious purpose of scientific research. In the past century, whalers have killed more than 100,000 minke whales in the southern hemisphere and most of these were probably Antarctic minkes.

Where to look

As its name suggests, the Antarctic minke whale
spends summer in the cold waters around Antarctica
– from about 55°S through the deep waters of the
Southern Ocean and right up to the ice edge. Little
is known about its seasonal migrations, but
most individuals probably spend the winter between
about 7°S and 35°S. A few may reach as far north as
the equator.

Antarctic minke whales, Antarctic Peninsula

Bryde's Whale
Balaenoptera edeni

ID FACT FILE

OTHER NAMES
Tropical whale.
MAXIMUM LENGTH
15.5 metres.
MAXIMUM WEIGHT
40 tonnes.
FIELD ID
Dark, smoky grey
upperside, white
underside
(upperside may
appear brown in
some lights);
skin may be
mottled; three
parallel
longitudinal
ridges on head;
prominent,
falcate fin;
narrow, hazy
blow; arches
back but does
not raise flukes
when diving.
DIET
Mainly small
schooling fish,
but also krill.
BREEDING
Calves every 2
years; gestation
about 12
months.

Bryde's whale is named after a
Norwegian called Johan Bryde, who was
a whaling pioneer in South Africa. The
least-known of the large baleen whales, it
is unusual because it does not seem to
migrate long distances between separate
feeding and breeding grounds every year.
It stays in warm waters, and may even eat
and breed in the same general area. In
the past Bryde's whales that were caught
by whalers were often mistakenly
recorded as sei whales, but they are
unique in having three longitudinal
ridges along the top of the head (all other
members of the family have just one).
The history of whaling for Bryde's whales
is largely unknown, because of the
confusion with sei whales, but in recent
years Japanese whalers have been taking
this species in the North Pacific. There
may be more than one species and,
indeed, it is likely that a pygmy form of
Bryde's whale will be assigned separate
species status in the near future.

Where to look

Bryde's whales are found in tropical to temperate
waters worldwide. Rarely moving farther north or
south than 40°, they occur both offshore and near
the coast. There seem to be specific pockets of
abundance where there is unusually high
productivity, such as off southern Africa and western
Australia. The pygmy form is known from the
eastern Indian Ocean, the western Pacific and
Australasia and may yet be found elsewhere.

Sei Whale
Balaenoptera borealis

ID FACT FILE

OTHER NAMES
Sardine whale,
pollack whale,
coalfish whale,
Rudolphi's
rorqual, finner.

MAXIMUM LENGTH
19 metres.

MAXIMUM WEIGHT
45 tonnes.

FIELD ID
Large, sleek
body; dark grey
upperside, white
or creamy
underside; often
has oval-shaped
scars; single
longitudinal ridge
on head; tall,
falcate fin; tall
columnar blow;
does not arch
back as much as
other whales or
raise flukes
when diving.

DIET
Broad range of
prey from small
schooling fish to
krill and
copepods.

BREEDING
Calves every 2–3
years; gestation
11–12 months.

The sei whale is poorly known. It lives far from shore, tends to be elusive and does not seem to gather in the same predictable areas year after year. There may be large numbers of sei whales in a particular region one year and then none for years or even decades afterwards. No commercial whale-watch operation relies on this species, for this reason, although it is sometimes encountered during tours specialising in humpbacks, minkes and other large whales. Named after a Norwegian word for the fish we call pollack, because the appearance of pollack off Norway's coast sometimes coincided with the arrival of sei whales, it is capable of swimming at up to 25 knots – making it one of the fastest of the large whales. For many years it was confused with the similar Bryde's whale, but the two species can be told apart by the number of longitudinal ridges along the tops of their heads.

Where to look

Found worldwide from tropical to cool temperate
waters. Most sei whales probably migrate between
cool summer feeding grounds and warm winter
breeding grounds. More than 200,000 were killed in
Antarctica in the past century and numbers there
remain greatly depleted. Unknown numbers were
killed elsewhere (whalers confused them with
Bryde's whales and anything vaguely resembling a
fin whale was often recorded merely as a 'finner').
Seis appear to be reasonably abundant in the North
Atlantic and North Pacific.

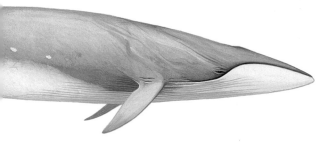

Fin Whale
Balaenoptera physalus

ID FACT FILE

OTHER NAMES
Finback, finner,
herring whale,
common rorqual,
razorback.

MAXIMUM LENGTH
27 metres.

MAXIMUM WEIGHT
120 tonnes.

FIELD ID
Exceptionally
large and sleek;
dark upperside,
light underside;
asymmetrical
head
pigmentation;
greyish-white
chevron; small,
backward-sloping
fin far down
back; single
longitudinal
ridge on
head; tall,
narrow blow;
rarely
raises
flukes
when
diving.

DIET
Schooling fish,
krill and other
crustaceans,
some squid
(mainly krill in
southern
hemisphere).

BREEDING
Calves every 2–3
years; gestation
11–12 months

The second largest animal on Earth, after
the blue whale, the fin whale is a sleek
and fast swimmer capable of reaching
speeds of over 25 knots. It is unusual in
having asymmetrical pigmentation on its
head – the lower jaw, mouth cavity and
some of the baleen plates are white on
the right side, but they are uniformly grey
or black on the left side. No one knows
the reason for such intriguing colouration,
but it may be an adaptation to confuse the
whale's small prey. Females are up to 10

per cent longer than males and southern
hemisphere animals can be 20 per cent
longer than their northern hemisphere
counterparts. So the average length for a
northern hemisphere male is 21 metres,
while the average for a southern
hemisphere female is 26 metres. Northern
and southern hemisphere populations do
not come into contact and may be
separate sub-species. Male and female fin
whales make very loud, low-frequency
vocalisations that can travel over hundreds
of kilometres in deep water.

Where to look

Found in tropical, temperate and polar regions
worldwide, but most common in cooler waters
offshore. Some populations seem to be resident
year-round, or make very short migrations, but
others travel between warm waters in winter and
cooler waters in summer. No distinct breeding or
calving grounds have been identified. The world
population was substantially reduced by commercial
whaling (three-quarters of a million were killed in
the southern hemisphere alone).

Blue Whale
Balaenoptera musculus

ID FACT FILE

OTHER NAMES
Sulphur-bottom,
Sibbald's rorqual,
great northern
rorqual.

MAXIMUM LENGTH
33.6 metres.

MAXIMUM WEIGHT
190 tonnes.

FIELD ID
Exceptionally
large; mottled
blue-grey; tiny,
stubby fin far
down back;
broad, flattened,
U-shaped head;
huge blowhole
splashguard;
single
longitudinal
ridge on head;
extremely thick
tailstock; very
tall blow; often
raises flukes
when diving.

DIET
Mainly krill,
occasionally
pelagic crabs.

BREEDING
Calves every 2–3
years; gestation
about 11
months.

The largest animal known to have lived
on Earth, the blue whale is almost as long
as a Boeing 737 and needs so much food
that, in terms of weight, it could eat a
fully-grown African elephant every day.
But its sheer size made it one of the most
sought-after species during the heyday of
whaling and it was hunted relentlessly
from the late nineteenth century until
beyond the middle of the twentieth
century. No fewer than 360,000 were
killed in Antarctic waters alone. Some
populations were reduced by 99 per cent
of their original numbers and it is likely
that they will never recover. Blue whales
possess the loudest voice in the animal
kingdom, emitting low-frequency sounds
that can travel literally hundreds of
kilometres in deep water. It is not known
whether these are for long-distance

communication or to assist with navigation and orientation. There is a sub-species known as the pygmy blue whale, which is particularly common in the Indian Ocean and may ultimately be recognised as a separate species.

Where to look
Worldwide from the tropics to the poles, although its distribution is very patchy. Some populations migrate long distances between low-latitude winter breeding grounds and high-latitude summer feeding grounds, but others appear to be resident. The only population that may be thriving today summers off the coasts of California and Mexico.

Sperm Whale
Physeter macrocephalus

ID FACT FILE

OTHER NAMES
Cachalot, great
sperm whale.

MAXIMUM LENGTH
11 metres
(female), 18
metres (male).

MAXIMUM WEIGHT
24 tonnes
(female), 57
tonnes (male).

FIELD ID
Dark body with
wrinkled skin;
huge, squarish
head; low hump
instead of fin;
'knuckles' from
hump to flukes;
single, slit-like
blowhole;
sideways,
forward-angled
blow; often lies
stationary at
surface; raises
flukes high when
diving.

DIET
Mainly squid, but
also octopuses,
sharks and other
fish.

BREEDING
Calves every 4–6
years (longer in
older females);
gestation 14–18
months.

With its disproportionately large head
and wrinkled skin, the sperm whale is
very distinctive. The largest of the
toothed whales, it dives deeper and for
longer than any other cetacean (with the
possible exception of some beaked
whales). No other cetacean shows such a
marked difference in size between the
sexes: males are almost twice as large as
females and lead very different lives.
Groups of females and immatures of both
sexes stay in the same general area for
many years, but adult males are generally
solitary and travel huge distances. In fact,
the males travel so far and wide that
populations around the world are very
similar genetically. The sperm whale was
the mainstay of the whaling industry for
many years, hunted mainly for its
spermaceti oil (a waxy oil found in the
head) and body oil. It is believed that
more than a million sperm whales were
killed over several centuries and the latest
population estimate suggests there could
be as few as 360,000 left.

Where to look

Patchy distribution worldwide from the tropics to
high latitudes near the edge of the pack ice. Sperm
whales are most common offshore and over
deepwater canyons, but can be found close to shore
if the water is sufficiently deep. Most females and
immature males live in temperate and tropical seas
at latitudes less than 40° (50° in the North Pacific).
Only the large adult males venture to the extreme
north and south of the range, where they feed.

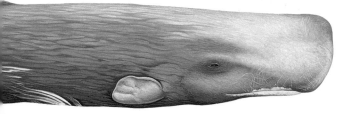

THE WHALE THAT THINKS IT IS A SUBMARINE

Sperm whales behave more like submarines than air-breathing mammals. Capable of diving well beyond the limits of almost any other mammal, they disappear into the cold, dark ocean depths to catch deepwater squid or sharks and other large fish.

They eat as much as a tonne of food every day, each prey animal ranging in size from a few centimetres to almost the length of the whales themselves. One individual was observed tackling a giant squid some 14.5 metres long, including its tentacles, while no fewer than 28,000 smaller squid were found in the stomach of another.

Scientists from the Woods Hole Oceanographic Institute recorded an incredible, record-breaking dive during a research study near the Caribbean island of Dominica. In 1991, they tagged a pair of male sperm whales and regularly tracked them at depths of 400–600 metres. On one occasion, though, the larger of the two whales made a breathtaking dive to a depth of 2,000 metres.

There is plenty of circumstantial evidence to suggest that sperm whales may be able to dive even deeper. On 25 August 1969, for example, a male sperm whale was killed by whalers 160 kilometres south of Durban, South Africa.

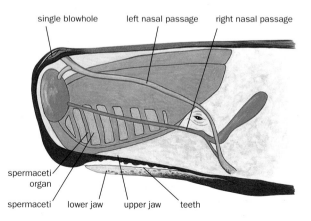

single blowhole   left nasal passage   right nasal passage

spermaceti organ

spermaceti   lower jaw   upper jaw   teeth

SPERM WHALE

Inside its stomach were two small sharks which, according to local experts, had been swallowed about an hour earlier; these were later identified as a particular kind of dogfish, found only on the seafloor. Since the water in that area exceeds a depth of 3,193 metres for a radius of some 48–64 kilometres, it is logical to assume that the sperm whale had been to a similar depth when hunting the two sharks.

Incidentally, the same whale also made one of the longest confirmed dives of any mammal. By the time it surfaced to breathe, having caught its prey, it had been underwater for an incredible one hour 52 minutes.

One explanation for such astonishing diving capabilities may lie in the sperm whale's enormous, barrel-shaped head. Much of the bulk of the head consists of a strange spongy tissue, known as the spermaceti organ, which is saturated with a yellowy wax. According to one theory, this could be used to control the whale's buoyancy in the water. By altering the temperature (and thus the density) of the wax the whale could sink or float with the minimum of effort. Another idea is that it cushions the animal's head during fights (heavy scarring and occasional broken teeth and jaws suggest serious skirmishes between males). But the most likely theory to explain the purpose of this massive oil-filled organ is that it works as an acoustic lens to channel sound emissions.

Dwarf Sperm Whale

Kogia sima

ID FACT FILE

OTHER NAMES
Owen's pygmy
sperm whale.

MAXIMUM LENGTH
2.7 metres.

MAXIMUM WEIGHT
275 kilograms.

FIELD ID
Small, robust
body; bluish-grey
upperside, dull
white or pinkish
underside;
squarish head
with underslung
lower jaw;
prominent,
falcate fin
midway along
back; false
'gill'; low,
inconspicuous
blow; floats
motionless at
surface; does
not raise flukes
when diving.

DIET
Mainly mid- and
deep-water
squid, some fish
and crustaceans.

BREEDING
May calve every
2 years or less;
gestation about
12 months.

Like their much larger and better-known relative, dwarf sperm whales have spermaceti organs in their heads and are deep divers. They are very similar in appearance to pygmy sperm whales and the two species are difficult to tell apart at sea, except in perfect conditions at very close range. They were separated as distinct species as recently as 1966. The dwarf sperm whale is slightly smaller (by about half a metre on average) and usually has a more prominent dorsal fin positioned farther forward on the back. Stranded individuals of both species have been mistaken for sharks because of their underslung lower jaws and the distinctive crescent-shaped markings on either side of the head between the eye and the flipper (which resemble gill-slits and have been dubbed 'false gills'). Dwarf sperm whales occur alone or in small groups of up to 10 animals of mixed age and sex. Both species are often seen lying motionless at the surface, with the back of the head exposed and the tail hanging down in the water. They can be approached quite closely, but then startle and dive.

DWARF SPERM WHALE

Where to look

Dwarf sperm whales are found worldwide in tropical
to temperate waters of the Atlantic, Pacific and
Indian Oceans, although they have never been
officially recorded across vast areas within this
assumed range. Some evidence suggests that the
dwarf sperm whale may prefer warmer, shallower
coastal waters than the pygmy sperm whale. There is
no evidence that the species migrates.

Pygmy Sperm Whale
Kogia breviceps

ID FACT FILE

OTHER NAMES
Lesser sperm whale, short-headed sperm whale, lesser cachalot.

MAXIMUM LENGTH
3.8 metres.

MAXIMUM WEIGHT
450 kilograms.

FIELD ID
Small, robust body; bluish-grey upperside, dull white or pinkish underside; squarish head with underslung lower jaw; falcate fin behind midline on body; false 'gill'; low, inconspicuous blow; floats motionless at surface; does not raise flukes when diving.

DIET
Mainly mid- and deep-water squid, some fish and crustaceans.

BREEDING
May calve every 2 years or less; gestation about 12 months.

Like the virtually identical dwarf sperm whale, the pygmy sperm whale is rarely encountered at sea except in a few well-known hotspots. Neither species appears to be particularly numerous, although they can be overlooked in anything but the calmest conditions and may be more common than the lack of evidence currently suggests. Both species are sometimes killed in Japan, Indonesia and the Lesser Antilles, and at least some are drowned in fishing nets. They are unusual among cetaceans in having a store of dark reddish-brown liquid in the lower intestines, which they expel into the water when they are startled – perhaps as a decoy, like the ink of a squid. They also have unusually-

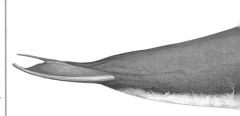

shaped heads, which appear square from the side and conical when viewed from above or below; they become blunter and squarer as the animals age. Pygmy sperm whales occur alone or in small groups of up to six animals of mixed age and sex.

Where to look
Pygmy sperm whales are found worldwide in tropical to temperate waters of the Atlantic, Pacific and Indian Oceans, although they have never been officially recorded across vast areas within this assumed range. Limited evidence suggests that the pygmy sperm whale prefers cooler, deeper waters seaward of the continental shelf. There is no evidence that the species migrates.

Narwhal
Monodon monoceros

ID FACT FILE

OTHER NAMES
Narwhale.
MAXIMUM LENGTH
4.7 metres.
MAXIMUM WEIGHT
1.6 tonnes.
FIELD ID
Long tusk of
male; mottled
black-and-white
back and sides;
low fleshy ridge
instead of fin;
short, rounded
head; slight hint
of beak; short,
upcurled flippers;
convex
'backward-facing'
flukes; inhabits
very high
latitudes; rarely
raises flukes
when diving.
DIET
Variety of fish,
squid and
crustaceans.
BREEDING
Calves every 2–3
years; gestation
about 15
months.

Centuries ago the male narwhal's long,
spiralling tusk was believed to be the
horn of the legendary unicorn and
traders selling it made huge profits by
keeping this distinctive whale's existence
a secret. Looking like a gnarled and
twisted walking stick, the tusk is actually
a modified tooth – the left of two upper
teeth, it pierces the lip and keeps
growing to a length of up to three
metres. A small number of males have
two tusks and, rarely, females grow them
as well. Their purpose is still a
matter of debate, but they
are certainly not used to
spear fish and may instead
be weapons in fights over
females or used as visual
displays of strength. Narwhals
are deep divers, capable of staying
underwater for as long as 20
minutes and reaching
depths of more

than 1,000 metres. They have been hunted for centuries by indigenous peoples for their meat and tusks and in some areas are threatened by oil and gas exploration and pollution. The total population is believed to be around 50,000.

Where to look

A truly Arctic species, the narwhal lives further north than almost any other cetacean. Found mostly above the Arctic Circle, and right to the edge of the permanent ice, it moves with the receding and expanding ice edge. It is most common on the North Atlantic side of the Arctic (especially Greenland and north-western Canada) and less common on the North Pacific side.

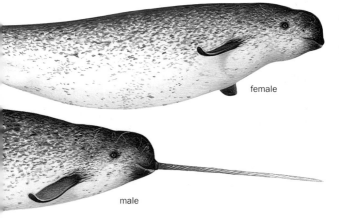

female

male

Beluga
Delphinapterus leucas

Ancient mariners used to call the
beluga the 'sea canary' because of its
great repertoire of trills, moos, clicks,
squeaks and twitters, which was once
described by a beluga scientist as
sounding like a string orchestra tuning
up before a concert. One of the most
vocal of all the toothed whales, it can
even be heard from above the surface.
Unlike most other cetaceans, it can
change the shape of its extraordinary
bulging head and is able to turn its head
from side to side or move it up and
down. Not all belugas are white: the
body colour changes with age, from
dark slate-grey at birth to pure white
(with dark lines along the dorsal ridge
and the edges of the flippers and flukes)

in adulthood. Known to dive to depths of at least 800 metres, belugas are believed to forage near the seabed. They have been hunted for centuries and pollution is a serious threat in some regions. The best population estimate is around 100,000.

Where to look

Belugas are found only in seasonally ice-covered waters of the sub-Arctic and Arctic. They occur mostly in shallow coastal waters, but will enter estuaries and even rivers. The largest population (accounting for 40 per cent of the total) lives in the Beaufort Sea, but they are more readily seen in eastern Canada's lower St Lawrence River and the Churchill River in western Hudson Bay.

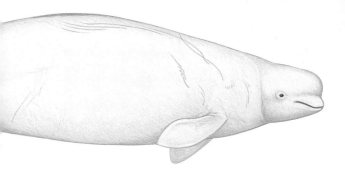

BEAKED WHALES

The beaked whales are the strangest and least known of all
the cetaceans. Several of them have never been seen alive
and the only evidence of their existence has been gleaned
from dead animals caught by fishermen or washed ashore.
Others are known from just a few brief encounters at sea, but
have never been photographed. Very few have been studied
in any detail.

There are currently 21 known species, all belonging to the
family Ziphiidae. But this figure is constantly under review as
new species are discovered and described. The most recent
addition to the list is Perrin's beaked whale, which was
formally named in 2002 and is known from just five animals
stranded along the coast of California. Another relatively new
species is Bahamonde's beaked whale, which was added to
the list in 1995; also known as the spade-toothed whale, this
whale was described from nothing more than part of a skull
found in the Juan Fernández Islands, off the coast of Chile.

Beaked whales are small- to medium-sized whales, ranging
in length from just under four metres to nearly 13 metres. As
their name suggests, the majority of them have pronounced

BEAKED WHALES

beaks, which are relatively shorter than in most dolphins but longer than in most whales. They also have a pair of distinctive throat grooves (in the shape of a 'V') and, unique among cetaceans, slight depressions called 'flipper pockets' where their small flippers can be tucked away alongside the body.

But their most remarkable feature is their teeth. There are no functional teeth in females or immature males (they do not erupt or are absent altogether) and there are only two or four functional teeth in the lower jaw of adult males. Shepherd's beaked whale is the main exception: both sexes have a full set of normal odontocete teeth in both the upper and lower jaws. Also, tiny teeth are present in the upper jaw of both sexes in Gray's beaked whales (embedded in the gum rather than the bone).

Observing and identifying beaked whales at sea can be extremely difficult. They usually live far from land and spend relatively little time at the surface between dives. More frustratingly, many species look remarkably alike from a distance. Relying on colour alone is virtually impossible for most species, since so little is known about the colouration of live animals and the little we do know suggests that there is tremendous variation between individuals. Normally there is no visible blow, and no beaked whales are known to lift their flukes when diving. In many cases, females are impossible to identify positively at sea unless they are accompanied by males.

However, more researchers have made an effort to study the enigmatic beaked whales in recent years and, although they are still shrouded in mystery, our knowledge has improved enormously.

Peruvian beaked whale skull

Sowerby's Beaked Whale
Mesoplodon bidens

ID FACT FILE

OTHER NAMES
North Sea beaked whale, North Atlantic beaked whale.

MAXIMUM LENGTH
5.5 metres.

MAXIMUM WEIGHT
1.3 tonnes.

FIELD ID
(Male only) Bluish-grey or slate-grey upperside, lighter underside; teeth mid-way along long, slender beak; slight bulge in front of blowhole; small falcate fin two-thirds of the way along back; limited scarring; usually unobtrusive behaviour; surfaces at steep angle.

DIET
Squid and some fish.

BREEDING
Calving interval and gestation period unknown.

Sowerby's beaked whale was the first of the beaked whales to be described – a male stranded in 1800 in the Moray Firth, north-eastern Scotland, and the skull was collected. A couple of years later, James Sowerby, an English watercolour artist, painted a picture of the skull and how he imagined the animal might have looked. Although its existence has been known for over two centuries, Sowerby's beaked whale is rarely encountered at sea and is still poorly known. It does occasionally strand, but basic natural history data such as stomach contents is still limited. The position of the teeth in the male is distinctive, lying mid-way between the tip of the beak and the corner of the

female

mouth, although they may be visible only at close range. Females are probably unidentifiable at sea. They are usually seen alone or in small groups of up to 10 animals of mixed sex and age and are capable of diving for at least half an hour.

Where to look

With one of the most northerly distributions of all beaked whales, this species is found mainly in cold temperate and sub-arctic waters of the northern North Atlantic. It appears to be most common in the east, especially in the northern North Sea. There are no known hunts, although Sowerby's beaked whale has been hunted in the past off Iceland and in the Barents Sea. Nothing is known about its abundance.

male

Andrews' Beaked Whale

Mesoplodon bowdoini

ID FACT FILE

OTHER NAMES
Bowdoin's beaked
whale, splay-
toothed beaked
whale, deepcrest
beaked whale.

MAXIMUM LENGTH
4.9 metres.

MAXIMUM WEIGHT
Possibly 1.5
tonnes.

FIELD ID
(Male only)
Robust
body; dark blue-
black colour;
white scratches
and scars; short,
thick beak
predominantly
white; strongly
arched mouthline;
teeth visible in
middle of beak;
small fin.

DIET
Probably squid
and some fish.

BREEDING
Calving interval
and gestation
period unknown.

Andrews' beaked whale is so similar in appearance and morphology to Hubbs' beaked whale that it has been suggested they belong to the same species. However, based on genetic evidence they are currently considered to be distinct species. Andrews' has never been

male

positively identified at sea, so everything we know about it has been inferred from strandings. These are relatively infrequent, suggesting that it is relatively rare. The male, in particular, is rather distinctive with a short, thick beak and a large tooth perched on the top of each side of its highly arched lower jaw. Linear body scarring on adult males is probably made by the teeth of other males. The species is named after a curator at the American Museum of Natural History in New York, Roy Chapman Andrews.

Where to look

Known only from strandings along the southern coast of Australia (including Tasmania) and New Zealand (including some sub-Antarctic islands), as well as oceanic islands such as the Falkland Islands and Tristan da Cunha. Such limited evidence suggests that Andrews' beaked whale has a circumpolar distribution in the southern hemisphere north of the Antarctic Convergence.

Hubbs' Beaked Whale

Mesoplodon carlhubbsi

Hubbs' beaked whale is another poorly-known member of the family and, again, most information comes from strandings. Adult males are covered in a remarkable number of single and double linear scars, which are probably made by the teeth of other males during aggressive encounters over females or dominance hierarchies. Other male beaked whales have similar scarring, but rarely as much as in this species. It is so similar in appearance and morphology to Andrews' beaked whale

male

that it has been suggested they belong to the same species. However, based on genetic evidence, they are currently considered to be distinct. Hubbs' beaked whale was named after the American ichthyologist Carl Hubbs – in 1945, a live specimen stranded outside his office at Scripps Institution of Oceanography, in California.

ID FACT FILE

OTHER NAMES
Arch-beaked whale.

MAXIMUM LENGTH
5.3 metres.

MAXIMUM WEIGHT
1.5 tonnes.

FIELD ID
(Male only) Dark, robust body; tangle of linear scars; raised white 'cap' on fairly bulbous melon; stocky, elongated beak mainly white; strongly arched lower jaw; massive teeth visible on top of arch in centre of beak; slightly falcate fin.

DIET
Squid and some fish.

BREEDING
Calving interval and gestation period unknown.

Where to look

Known only from temperate waters in the North Pacific, Hubbs' beaked whale appears to be most common along the California coast and north into British Columbia. It may occur as far south as the Pacific coast of Baja California, Mexico. However, it has also been recorded in Japan (along the north-eastern coast of the main island of Honshu) and therefore may range right across the North Pacific.

Blainville's Beaked Whale

Mesoplodon densirostris

ID FACT FILE

OTHER NAMES
Tropical beaked whale, dense-beaked whale, Atlantic beaked whale.

MAXIMUM LENGTH
4.9 metres.

MAXIMUM WEIGHT
1 tonne.

FIELD ID
(Male only) Dark upperside, lighter underside; fairly prominent fin two-thirds of the way along back; strongly-arched lower jaw; thick, moderately long beak; huge, horn-like teeth; flattened forehead; many oval scars, some scratching.

DIET
Squid and octopuses.

BREEDING
Calving interval and gestation period unknown.

Blainville's beaked whale has a wider distribution than almost any other known beaked whale, but sightings are still relatively rare. Most of our knowledge comes from dead animals washed ashore – it often strands on oceanic islands on both sides of the equator – and from observations on live animals in just three key hotspots. However, it was one of the first beaked whales to be identified when, in 1817, Henri de Blainville managed to describe it from a small piece of jaw. His specimen was the heaviest bone structure he had ever seen (denser even than elephant ivory) and this gave rise to its other common name: the dense-beaked whale. The male has a distinctive, high-arched jawline, with two large teeth on the crest that grow forward and protrude from both sides of the closed mouth. The teeth are not always

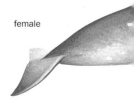

female

visible, though, as they can be obscured by stalked barnacles. Blainville's beaked whales make deep dives for food that can last for up to 45 minutes.

Where to look
Mainly found in tropical to warm temperate waters worldwide, especially in deep water and around gullies on the continental slope. Occasional records in higher latitudes may be linked to warm water currents. There are only three areas where Blainville's beaked whale is observed on a regular basis: the north-eastern Bahamas; Oahu, Hawaii; and Moorea in the Society Islands of the South Pacific.

male

Perrin's Beaked Whale

Mesoplodon perrini

Perrin's beaked whale is the most recent addition to the cetacean list, and was described for the first time in 2002. It is known from just five animals which stranded along the coast of California between 1975 and 1997. There was considerable confusion over their identification at first, and four were initially identified as Hector's beaked whales and the fifth as Cuvier's beaked whale. However, after detailed genetic studies, beaked whale experts realised they belonged to a new species. It now seems likely that sightings of two small beaked whales off California in 1976 and 1978, which were identified as Hector's beaked whales, are more likely to have been Perrin's. There are subtle differences between the two species. Perrin's beaked whale was named after W. F. Perrin, who collected two of the known specimens.

male

Where to look

Known only from five strandings in California, between Torrey Pines State Reserve just north of San Diego and Fisherman's Wharf in Monterey, suggesting a range in the eastern North Pacific. However, this is very limited evidence and it is possible that the true distribution is much broader. Like other beaked whales, it is likely to be found in oceanic waters deeper than 1,000 metres.

Hector's Beaked Whale
Mesoplodon hectori

Until recently, information about Hector's beaked whale was confusing. It was known mostly from stranded animals in two widely separated parts of the world: in the southern hemisphere and many thousands of kilometres away along the coast of California. But the four animals stranded in California between 1975 and 1997 (originally identified as Hector's beaked whales) are now known to be a recently-described species,

male

Perrin's beaked whale. Hector's beaked whale has never been reliably identified alive in the wild. Very little is known about its abundance, but it is generally considered to be one of the rarer beaked whales. Like Hector's dolphin, this species was named after the curator of the colonial museum in Wellington, New Zealand: Sir James Hector.

ID FACT FILE

OTHER NAMES
New Zealand beaked whale, skew-beaked whale.

MAXIMUM LENGTH
4.2 metres.

MAXIMUM WEIGHT
Unknown.

FIELD ID
(Male only) Dark upperside, lighter underside; small, spindle-shaped body; large, slightly triangular teeth on tip of lower jaw; small, triangular and slightly falcate dorsal fin two-thirds of the way along back.

DIET
Probably squid and some fish.

BREEDING
Calving interval and gestation period unknown.

Where to look

Most records of Hector's beaked whale are from New Zealand, but it seems to have a circumpolar distribution in cool, temperate waters of the southern hemisphere. There are also records from Chile, Argentina, the Falkland Islands, South Africa and Tasmania. Earlier records of Hector's beaked whales in the northern hemisphere are now known to be Perrin's beaked whale.

Gervais' Beaked Whale

Mesoplodon europaeus

ID FACT FILE

OTHER NAMES
Gulf Stream
beaked whale,
Antillean beaked
whale, European
beaked whale.

MAXIMUM LENGTH
5.2 metres.

MAXIMUM WEIGHT
1.5 tonnes.

FIELD ID
(Male only)
Medium-sized,
slender body;
dark grey
upperside, paler
grey underside;
spindle-shaped
body; some
linear scarring;
fairly long,
narrow beak;
teeth barely
visible a third of
the way back
from tip of jaw;
small fin two-
thirds of the way
down back.

DIET
Probably squid
and some fish.

BREEDING
Calving interval
and gestation
period unknown.

Gervais' beaked whale is another poorly-known member of the family that has never been reliably identified alive at sea. Consequently, nearly everything we know about its distribution, abundance and natural history has been gleaned from a relatively small number of strandings. The type specimen (used to describe the species) was found floating dead in the English Channel in 1840 – hence it was scientifically named *Mesoplodon europaeus* in 1855 and, for a while at least, dubbed the European beaked whale. However, most records are from warmer waters further south, along the Atlantic coast of North America, in the

Caribbean and in the Gulf of Mexico. Intriguingly, a count of tooth layers in one particular stranded individual suggests that it was at least 27 years old.

Where to look
Deep tropical and warm temperate waters in the western North Atlantic, with scattered records in the eastern North Atlantic: western Africa, the Canary Islands and Ireland. It is also known from Ascension Island, in the South Atlantic. There is no information on its abundance, although it does strand along the Atlantic coast of North America (especially in Florida) more than any other *Mesoplodon* species.

male

female

Ginkgo-toothed Beaked Whale

Mesoplodon ginkgodens

The ginkgo-toothed beaked whale is named for the male's strangely flattened teeth, which are shaped like the leaves of a ginkgo tree – a common tree in Japan, where the first specimen of this whale was found and described in 1958. These teeth are about 10 centimetres wide, making them the widest of any known *Mesoplodon* species. The ginkgo-toothed beaked whale has never been identified alive at sea and is very poorly known. Most information comes from stranded animals found on shore and a handful of individuals killed by Japanese whalers. Unlike many of its relatives, the male has very few (if any) linear scars on its body – suggesting that males do not fight over dominance hierarchies or females. However, males do have white spots and blotches, especially around the navel, which may be parasitic scars rather than true pigmentation.

Where to look
This species is known only from a small number of widely-scattered records in the tropical and warm temperate waters of the Pacific and Indian Oceans, from Japan and California to the Galapagos Islands and the Maldives. The ginkgo-toothed beaked whale was being hunted on an opportunistic basis by shore-based whalers in Japan and Taiwan even before it had been scientifically described. There is no information on abundance.

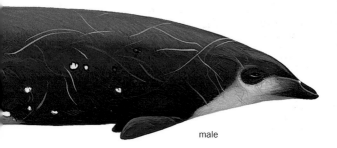

male

Gray's Beaked Whale

Mesoplodon grayi

ID FACT FILE

OTHER NAMES
Haast's beaked
whale,
scamperdown
whale, southern
beaked whale,
small-toothed
beaked whale.

MAXIMUM LENGTH
5.6 metres.

MAXIMUM WEIGHT
1.3 tonnes.

FIELD ID
(Male only)
Slender, spindle-
shaped body;
dark upperside,
lighter underside;
very long,
slender,
predominantly
white beak;
slightly bulging
melon; small,
triangular teeth
visible about a
third of way back
from tip of beak;
small, falcate fin
two-thirds of the
way along back.

DIET
Probably squid
and some fish.

BREEDING
Calving interval
and gestation
period unknown.

Gray's beaked whales are among the
better-known *Mesoplodon* species.
Named in 1876 after John Edward Gray,
a zoologist at the British Museum, they
seem to be more active at the surface
than other beaked whales and are among
the few that have been photographed
alive at sea. This species is unique in the
Mesoplodon genus because adults of both
sexes have 34–44 tiny, evenly-spaced
teeth in the upper jaw. Adult males also
have two teeth on the lower jaw. Like the
other beaked whales with especially long
beaks, they often lift their beaks out of
the water at an angle of about 45 degrees
when surfacing. Although
normally encountered
or stranded

in small groups of up to eight animals, in 1874 there
was a mass stranding of 28 in the Chatham Islands,
east of New Zealand. This species is believed to be
one of the most gregarious members of the family.

Where to look
Gray's beaked whale has a circumpolar distribution
in temperate waters of the southern hemisphere,
mainly in the Southern Ocean south of 30°S. There
is a single record from the northern hemisphere – a
stranding in the Netherlands in 1927 – but this is
believed to have been exceptional and well outside
the normal range. The high number of strandings
suggests that it is fairly common and widespread.

male

female

Strap-toothed Whale

Mesoplodon layardii

ID FACT FILE

OTHER NAMES
Layard's beaked whale.

MAXIMUM LENGTH
6.2 metres.

MAXIMUM WEIGHT
1.5 tonnes.

FIELD ID
(Male only)
Strong dark and light markings; considerable body scarring; small fin two-thirds of the way along back; teeth curled around upper jaw; long, slender beak; slightly bulging melon; dark face 'mask'; beak may break surface first; difficult to approach.

DIET
Squid.

BREEDING
Calving interval and gestation period unknown.

The male strap-toothed whale is the largest member of the *Mesoplodon* genus. It has two extraordinary teeth which grow from its lower jaw, curl upwards and backwards and then extend over the top of its upper jaw. In older animals, they sometimes meet in the middle, forming a muzzle and preventing the whale from opening its jaws more than a few centimetres. The teeth may act as 'guard-rails', helping the whale to catch squid, its main prey, while it uses its mouth to suck like a vacuum cleaner. But this would not explain why such 'wrap-around' teeth are absent in females. A more likely explanation is that the teeth are a sexual characteristic, perhaps used in fighting or in some other way to determine the fittest males for mating. The variety of tooth formations originally led to the naming of at least four new species, but scientists now recognise that they are in fact all the same species. The strap-toothed whale was described by John Edward Gray, in 1865, from drawings sent by a curator of the South African Museum called E. L. Layard – thus its alternative name.

Where to look

The strap-toothed whale has a wide distribution in cool temperate waters of the southern hemisphere, roughly between 30°S and the Antarctic Convergence. It has stranded on beaches in Chile, Argentina, Uruguay, the Falkland Islands, southern Africa, New Zealand and Australia; although poorly known, it appears to be relatively common.

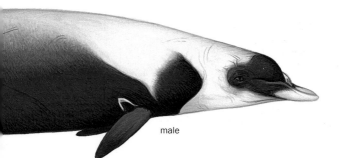

male

True's Beaked Whale

Mesoplodon mirus

ID FACT FILE

OTHER NAMES
Wonderful
beaked whale.
MAXIMUM LENGTH
5.3 metres.
MAXIMUM WEIGHT
1.4 tonnes.
FIELD ID
(Male only)
Rotund body;
dark upperside,
light underside
(white tail, fin
and flukes in
southern
hemisphere);
slightly bulbous
melon; medium-
sized beak; small
teeth at tip of
lower jaw; dark
patch around
eye; linear
scarring; fin two-
thirds of the way
along back.
DIET
Probably squid
and some fish.
BREEDING
Calving interval
and gestation
period unknown.

The distribution of True's beaked whale
has puzzled scientists for some time. It
has two widely separate populations, in
the North Atlantic and the southern
Indian Ocean, and there have been no
sightings or strandings in the huge gap in
between. The two populations are also
quite different in appearance. The
southern hemisphere form has an all-
white tail stock, dorsal fin and flukes,
which is absent in the North Atlantic
form. But it is still unclear
whether
these are
separate
sub-species or
even species. There have
been a few reliable sightings of True's
beaked whales at sea: most notably, a
group of three whales (believed to be two
adult females and a large calf) off
Hatteras Inlet, North Carolina. In July
2001, a single male was observed
breaching 24 times 50 kilometres
north of the
Spanish
coast in the
southern
Bay of Biscay. The
species was described in 1913
by American biologist Frederick
W. True, who named it *mirus*
(meaning 'wonderful').

Where to look

There are two apparently separate populations
of True's beaked whale. One lives in the warm
temperate waters of the North Atlantic (strandings
have been recorded mainly along the east coast of
the US and Canada, but also in Ireland, France,
Spain, the Canary Islands and the Azores). The
other is in the southern Indian Ocean, with
strandings in South Africa and Australia.

male

female

Stejneger's Beaked Whale
Mesoplodon stejnegeri

For nearly a century, the only evidence for the existence of Stejneger's beaked whale came from a single skull found on Bering Island, in the mid-nineteenth century. But since the late 1970s information about this enigmatic whale has improved and there are now more specimens available for study. In particular, in 1994 a group of four adult females stranded in the Aleutian Islands – providing the first Stejneger's beaked whales in good condition. The male has extraordinary tusk-like teeth, second only in size to the teeth of strap-toothed whales, which are set about 20 centimetres from the tip of the jaw immediately in front of the apex. They are laterally compressed and tilt forwards, sometimes converging towards one another and cutting into the upper lip. The species was named in 1855 after the man who found the first skull, Leonhard Stejneger.

Where to look

Cool temperate and sub-arctic waters of the North
Pacific (from California to Japan) and in the south-
western Bering Sea. Stejneger's may also range into
warm temperate waters, but the only evidence
for this is the presence of scars inflicted by cookie-
cutter sharks (the sharks are more abundant in
warmer waters further south).

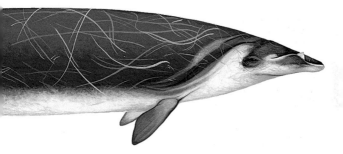

The Aleutian Islands may be a key centre of
distribution and there appears to be a distinct
population in the Sea of Japan.

Pygmy Beaked Whale

Mesoplodon peruvianus

ID FACT FILE

OTHER NAMES
Peruvian beaked whale, lesser beaked whale.

MAXIMUM LENGTH
3.9 metres.

MAXIMUM WEIGHT
Unknown.

FIELD ID
(Male only) Small size; spindle-shaped body; dark upperside, lighter underside; linear scarring; slightly bulbous melon; slightly sloping forehead; small beak with slightly arched jaw; teeth just visible in front of arch; small, triangular fin two-thirds of the way along back.

DIET
Fish and probably squid.

BREEDING
Calving interval and gestation period unknown.

The pygmy beaked whale is the smallest member of the family and one of the most recent cetacean species to be named. Scientists first became aware of its existence in 1976, when a skull was discovered at a fish market near San Andrés, in Peru. The first complete specimen (a female) was found in 1985, at another fish market just south of Lima, in Peru, and the first adult male was found three years later. In 1990, there were two strandings in La Paz Bay, Baja California, Mexico – the first outside Peruvian waters. The new species was officially named in 1991. Since then, it has been reliably identified at sea on several occasions, but almost nothing is known about its social structure or behaviour. There is also no information on abundance, but because many of the first specimens had been caught by fishermen off the coast of Peru, it raises alarm bells about what appears to be a high level of incidental catch.

Where to look

Limited records suggest mid- to deep waters in the
eastern tropical and temperate Pacific, mainly off
the coasts of Peru and Chile, but extending from
northern Mexico or southern California to northern
Chile. However, the range may be more extensive as
there is also a possible record – a stranding – from
New Zealand.

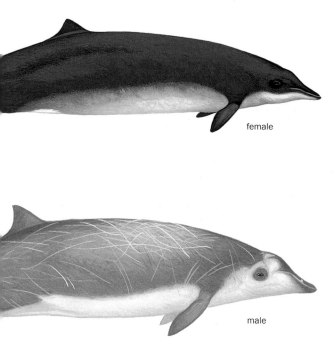

female

male

Bahamonde's Beaked Whale

Mesoplodon traversii

ID FACT FILE

OTHER NAMES
Spade-toothed
whale.
MAXIMUM LENGTH
Possibly 5.5
metres (based
on skull size).
MAXIMUM WEIGHT
Unknown.
FIELD ID
Similarities
in skull
characteristics
suggest that it
may be closely
related to
Andrews' beaked
whale and,
consequently, may
be similar in
appearance.
DIET
Probably squid
and fish.
BREEDING
Calving interval
and gestation
period unknown.

Part of a strange skull, belonging to an immature beaked whale, was found on Robinson Crusoe Island, in the Juan Fernández islands off Chile, in June 1986. After nearly a decade of painstaking examination by some of the world's leading beaked whale experts, it was officially named in 1995 as a species new to science. Since then, it has been discovered that two more specimens (part of a skull from New Zealand and an old tooth and jaw from the Chatham Islands) are genetically identical to the Chilean skull. It is possible that Bahamonde's beaked whale and the so-called 'unidentified beaked whale', known only from sightings in the Eastern Tropical Pacific, belong to the same species – but until complete specimens are found this is merely conjecture. The scientific name has recently been changed from *Mesoplodon bahamondi*.

Bahamonde's beaked
whale skull

Where to look

Currently known only from the Juan Fernández Archipelago, some 590 kilometres to the west of mainland Chile, and New Zealand (including the Chatham Islands). This would suggest a range across the South Pacific, but there is far too little evidence to be certain.

Shepherd's Beaked Whale

Tasmacetus shepherdi

Shepherd's beaked whale is the only member of the family with a full set of functional teeth in both jaws (Gray's beaked whale has tiny, vestigial teeth in the upper jaw). These occur in both sexes, though only the male has a pair of enlarged teeth at the tip of the lower jaw as in other beaked whales. Since most records are based on partly-decomposed animals washed ashore, there is little information on its appearance.

male

Shepherd's beaked whale was described by W. B. B. Oliver in 1937 from a nearly complete skeleton collected by a curator at the Wanganui Alexander Museum in New Zealand, G. Shepherd.

Where to look

Shepherd's beaked whales are known from strandings in New Zealand, the Chatham Islands, Australia, Argentina, the Juan Fernández Islands off Chile, Tristan da Cunha and the South Sandwich Islands. More than half of these were in New Zealand. Assuming that a sighting in the Seychelles was exceptional, this limited evidence suggests that it may be circumpolar in cool temperate waters between 33°S and 50°S.

ID FACT FILE

OTHER NAMES
Tasman beaked whale, Tasman whale.

MAXIMUM LENGTH
7 metres.

MAXIMUM WEIGHT
Unknown.

FIELD ID
(Male only)
Moderately large, spindle-shaped body; dark upperside, light patches on sides, underside and tail stock; light patch on bulbous melon; long, narrow, pointed beak with small teeth on tip; small, slightly falcate fin two-thirds of the way along back.

DIET
Probably squid and fish in equal quantities.

BREEDING
Calving interval and gestation period unknown.

Longman's Beaked Whale

Indopacetus pacificus

ID FACT FILE

OTHER NAMES
Pacific beaked
whale, Indo-
Pacific beaked
whale.

MAXIMUM LENGTH
Possibly 8
metres
(Maldivian
female 5.9
metres).

MAXIMUM WEIGHT
Unknown.

FIELD ID
Relatively large
size; brownish
upperside, lighter
underside;
bulbous melon;
visible low, bushy
blow; moderately
long, stubby
beak; two teeth
near tip of lower
jaw (presumably
erupting in male
only); falcate fin
two-thirds of the
way along back.

DIET
Probably squid
and fish.

BREEDING
Calving interval
and gestation
period unknown.

Until recently, Longman's beaked whale was one of the least-known cetaceans. The only evidence for its existence came from two weathered skulls: one discovered in 1882 on a beach near MacKay, in Queensland, Australia, and the other in 1955 on the floor of a fertiliser factory in Mogadishu, Somalia (later traced to a beach near Danane, where it had been picked up by a local fisherman). But in recent years four new specimens have been found: two juvenile males stranded on the Indian Ocean coast of South Africa, an adult female stranded in the Maldives, and a skull found in Kenya. Unfortunately, there is still no adult male available for study. However, in the past couple of years there have been some reliable

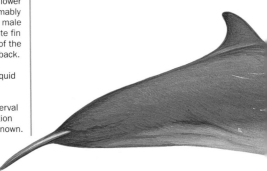

sightings of Longman's beaked whales at sea
(especially in the Maldives); and large beaked
whales occasionally reported from the warmer
waters of the Indian and Pacific Oceans – and
dubbed 'tropical bottlenose whales' – are now
believed to have been Longman's. The species is
named after Heber Longman, a curator at the
Queensland Museum, Australia, who recognised
the 1882 skull as belonging to a new species.

Where to look
Based on limited evidence from just six specimens
and a small number of reliable sightings at sea,
Longman's beaked whale appears to be distributed
in the western reaches of the tropical Pacific
Ocean and in the western, northern and southern
tropical Indian Ocean. 'Tropical bottlenose
whales' have been reported throughout the
tropical Indo-Pacific.

Cuvier's Beaked Whale

Ziphius cavirostris

ID FACT FILE

OTHER NAMES
Goose-beaked
whale.

MAXIMUM LENGTH
6.9 metres.

MAXIMUM WEIGHT
3 tonnes.

FIELD ID
(Male only)
Rotund body;
small head
shaped like
goose's beak;
white head;
small teeth at tip
of jaw; small,
falcate fin set
about two-thirds
along back; low,
inconspicuous
blow; long and
circular scars;
usually alone or
in small groups.

DIET
Mainly squid, but
sometimes fish
and possibly
crustaceans.

BREEDING
Calving interval
and gestation
period unknown.

When Cuvier's beaked whale was first described by the French anatomist Georges Cuvier, in 1823, it was believed to be extinct. However, it is now known to be one of the most abundant and widespread of the beaked whales and is one of the three most-watched members of the family (along with Baird's beaked whale and the northern bottlenose whale). The shape of its head and beak is sometimes described as resembling a goose's beak, which explains its alternative name, the goose-beaked whale. Cuvier's beaked whales vary enormously in colour, but are among the few ziphiids that can be readily identified at sea. Older males, in particular, are often heavily scarred from the teeth of other males and from bites by cookie-cutter sharks. The two teeth erupt only in males and can be

male

female

seen protruding from the tip of the lower jaw, even
when the mouth is closed; they sometimes have
stalked barnacles growing on them. Cuvier's beaked
whales strand more than any other member of the
beaked whale family.

Where to look
Widely distributed from the tropics to cool
temperate waters worldwide, Cuvier's beaked
whales seem to have very specific habitat
requirements – deep waters on the steepest portion
of the continental slope. It is difficult to predict
sightings, but a few of the hotspots where they
are sometimes seen on whale-watch trips include
the Bay of Biscay, the Canary Islands, the
Mediterranean and Hawaii.

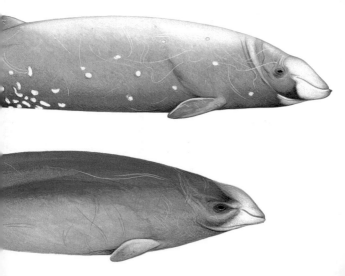

Baird's Beaked Whale
Berardius bairdii

ID FACT FILE

OTHER NAMES
Giant bottlenose whale, four-toothed whale.

MAXIMUM LENGTH
12.8 metres.

MAXIMUM WEIGHT
12 tonnes.

FIELD ID
Large size; long, dark grey, spindle-shaped body; extensive scarring on older animals; small fin two-thirds of the way along back; prominent, bulbous forehead sloping to long beak; anterior teeth may appear white in bright sunlight; tightly-packed groups.

DIET
Squid and fish.

BREEDING
Calves every 3 years or more; gestation possibly as long as 17 months.

The largest member of the family, Baird's beaked whale is very similar to Arnoux's beaked whale. These two species are unusual in having four teeth which erupt in both males and females: one large pair at the tip of the protruding lower jaw and a smaller pair just behind them. Baird's beaked whale was discovered in 1882 when researcher Leonhard Stejneger picked up a four-toothed skull on Bering Island. He published his discovery the following year and named the new species after his colleague, Spencer Baird, who had just been appointed Secretary of the Smithsonian Institution. Like other members of the family, Baird's beaked whales are deep divers. They can probably hold their breath for an hour or more, but most dives last around half an hour;

they are believed to reach depths of at least 1,000 metres on a regular basis. They are usually shy of vessels and difficult to approach, but can be active at the surface and have been observed spyhopping and breaching. The status of Baird's beaked whales is uncertain, but the world population is possibly in the order of a few tens of thousands.

Where to look
Deep temperate and sub-arctic waters in the North Pacific, especially around submarine escarpments and seamounts. Baird's beaked whales are rarely found close to shore, unless the continental shelf is exceptionally narrow. They have been hunted by the Japanese for centuries and 50–60 are still killed every year under a government quota system, mainly in the waters off the Boso Peninsula, near Tokyo, and off Hokkaido Island in the north.

Arnoux's Beaked Whale

Berardius arnuxii

ID FACT FILE

OTHER NAMES
Southern beaked whale, four-toothed whale, giant bottlenose whale, New Zealand beaked whale.

MAXIMUM LENGTH
9.8 metres.

MAXIMUM WEIGHT
Unknown.

FIELD ID
Large size; long, dark grey, spindle-shaped body; extensive linear scarring on older animals; bulbous melon; long, dolphin-like beak; teeth at tip of lower jaw may appear white in bright sunlight; small fin two-thirds of the way along back.

DIET
Squid and fish.

BREEDING
May calve every 3 years; gestation possibly as long as 17 months.

Arnoux's beaked whale is a very poorly-known whale, resembling Baird's beaked whale so closely that for many years it was uncertain whether Baird's represented a geographically isolated form of Arnoux's. But recent genetic studies seem to have settled the dispute in favour of two separate species. The main visible difference appears to be in size: Arnoux's is slightly smaller than Baird's. The two beaked whales would probably be indistinguishable at sea, although their ranges do not appear to overlap and it is highly unlikely that they would ever come into contact with one another. They are among the least sexually dimorphic members of the family – both males and females have erupted teeth and look remarkably similar. Named after a French surgeon, M. Arnoux, who presented the first skull to the Paris Museum of Natural History in 1846, Arnoux's beaked whale is usually shy and difficult to observe.

Where to look
Arnoux's beaked whales appear to inhabit vast areas of the southern hemisphere, from the Antarctic to southern Brazil, South Georgia, South Africa, New Zealand and Australia. Most records are south of 40°S from temperate to Antarctic waters. They are not known in the tropics. There is no information on abundance but, unlike its northern hemisphere relative, Arnoux's beaked whale is not taken by commercial whalers.

Northern Bottlenose Whale

Hyperoodon ampullatus

ID FACT FILE

OTHER NAMES
North Atlantic bottlenosed whale, flathead, bottlehead, steephead.

MAXIMUM LENGTH
9.8 metres.

MAXIMUM WEIGHT
7.5 tonnes.

One of the three most-watched members of the family (along with Cuvier's beaked whale and Baird's beaked whale), the northern bottlenose whale is a curious animal and frequently approaches stationary or slow-moving boats. Its most distinctive feature is its huge bulbous

forehead, which is particularly prominent in older males. There are two teeth at the tip of the lower jaw (erupting in males only) which are sometimes covered in stalked barnacles. Capable of diving to depths of 1,500 metres, it can remain submerged for over an hour. Hunted more than any other beaked whale, it has now been protected for more than 25 years.

FIELD ID
(Male only) Long, robust, cylindrical body; dark, yellow-brown upperside, lighter underside; bulbous melon often pale and squared-off; prominent beak; teeth at tip rarely visible; falcate fin; visible, bushy blow; may be curious.

DIET
Mainly squid, some fish, crustaceans and invertebrates.

BREEDING Calves every 2-3 years; gestation about 12 months.

Where to look

Lives in the cooler waters of the North Atlantic, mainly north of the Iberian Peninsula in the east and Nova Scotia in the west. It prefers deep water, especially beyond the continental shelf and over submarine canyons. Little is known about its seasonal movements – for instance, it appears to be present year-round in the Gully (a submarine canyon off Nova Scotia) but only during the summer in the southern Bay of Biscay.

Southern Bottlenose Whale

Hyperoodon planifrons

The southern bottlenose whale is quite poorly known. It lives far from shipping lanes, and has never been heavily exploited, so most information comes from strandings and incidental observations by researchers studying other species. It is not particularly difficult to identify at sea, although it does look similar to Arnoux's beaked whale from a distance and the two species have almost identical ranges.

The chocolatey yellow-brown colour is believed to be caused by a thin layer of diatoms (single-celled algae) as well as by natural pigmentation. They are usually found in small groups (one to four individuals is typical, although up to 20 have been observed together). Abundance estimates for the region south of the Antarctic Convergence in summer suggest a population of about 500,000.

Where to look

Found throughout the cold, deep waters of the southern hemisphere, from the Antarctic ice edge to about 30°S (with occasional sightings further north, especially in winter). Limited evidence suggests that there are seasonal movements, at least in some populations: the highest density, for instance, occurs during summer within about 100 kilometres of the Antarctic ice edge.

ID FACT FILE

OTHER NAMES
Antarctic bottlenosed whale, flathead.

MAXIMUM LENGTH
7.5 metres.

MAXIMUM WEIGHT
Unknown.

FIELD ID
(Male only) Long, robust body; dark, yellow-brown upperside, light underside; can look white at sea; bulbous melon, pale and squared-off; stubby beak; tiny teeth at tip; visible, bushy blow; prominent, falcate fin.

DIET
Squid, some fish and benthic invertebrates.

BREEDING
Possibly calves every 2-3 years; gestation may be about 12 months.

Pygmy Killer Whale
Feresa attenuata

ID FACT FILE

OTHER NAMES
Lesser killer whale, slender blackfish, slender pilot whale.

MAXIMUM LENGTH
2.6 metres.

MAXIMUM WEIGHT
170 kilograms.

FIELD ID
Robust, dark-coloured body; slightly paler grey sides, white patch on underside; dark dorsal cape visible in some light conditions; rounded head with no beak and white lips; some individuals have white chin; prominent falcate fin.

DIET
Mostly fish and squid.

BREEDING
Calving interval and gestation period unknown.

Although no bigger than a dolphin itself, the pygmy killer whale is known to attack other small cetaceans in the wild and has been quite aggressive towards other species and even people in captivity. Although it is widely distributed, it is not particularly well known. There are reports of bow-riding and wake-riding, but it tends to be less active than most oceanic dolphins and usually avoids boats. Schools often swim abreast in long 'chorus lines' and, when alarmed, bunch together – often leaping clear of the water in their determination to rush away. When viewed at close range, it is possible to see a distinctive white chin on some individuals and the white lips that are common in this species. It is similar in size to many oceanic dolphins, though is most likely to be confused with the

similar-looking melon-headed whale: generally
speaking, if a small number of animals are seen
together (fewer than 50) they are more likely to be
pygmy killer whales.

Where to look
Found worldwide in deep, offshore waters mainly in
the tropics and sub-tropics but also in warm
temperate regions, the pygmy killer whale rarely
occurs close to shore except around oceanic islands.
Small numbers are drowned in fishing nets and
caught up in drive fisheries in Japan, Sri Lanka and
elsewhere, and in several countries (especially in
Asia) it is harpooned opportunistically.

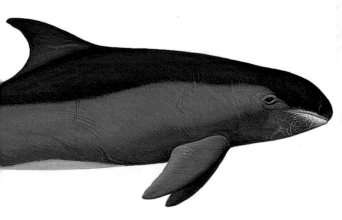

Melon-headed Whale
Peponocephala electra

ID FACT FILE

OTHER NAMES
Little killer
whale, electra
dolphin, many-
toothed
blackfish.
MAXIMUM LENGTH
2.7 metres.
MAXIMUM WEIGHT
210 kilograms.
FIELD ID
Small, torpedo-
shaped body;
overall dark grey
or black colour,
some white on
underside; dark
dorsal cape and
facial markings
visible in certain
lights; slim,
pointed head
(from above);
little or no beak;
white, light grey
or pink lips;
large, falcate fin.
DIET
Mostly fish and
squid, some
crustaceans.
BREEDING
Calving interval
unknown;
gestation
possibly about
12 months.

There seems to have been some
confusion over the melon-headed
whale's common name. The scientific
word *Peponocephala* was believed to
mean 'melon-headed' – 'pepo' was
thought to be Latin for 'melon' – and so
was used to describe the distinctively-
shaped, pointed head of this species.
But it has since transpired that 'pepo'
probably means 'pumpkin' – so, strictly-
speaking, it should be the pumpkin-
headed whale instead. Despite its wide
distribution, it is infrequently
encountered at sea except at certain
hotspots such as the
Maldives, Cebu
Island in the
Philippines,
Hawaii and off
the east coast of
Australia. It often creates a
lot of spray as it surfaces, and
frequently changes direction
underwater, making it difficult to see in
any detail. Confusion is most likely with
the pygmy killer whale, which is very
similar in appearance: generally
speaking, if there are several hundred
animals together they are more likely to
be melon-headed whales. Also, unlike
pygmy killer whales, they are
sometimes encountered in mixed
schools with Fraser's dolphins.

Where to look

Mainly found in deep, sub-tropical and tropical waters worldwide, the melon-headed whale is most common between about 20°N and 20°S. It is sometimes observed in temperate regions, though these are probably strays travelling in warm currents. Melon-headed whales are usually encountered offshore, and rarely venture close to shore except around oceanic islands or where the water is deep. Some drown in fishing nets and they are harpooned throughout their range.

False Killer Whale

Pseudorca crassidens

ID FACT FILE

OTHER NAMES
False pilot whale, pseudorca.

MAXIMUM LENGTH
6 metres.

MAXIMUM WEIGHT
2 tonnes.

FIELD ID
Relatively long and slender body; uniformly dark except for light areas on throat and chest; slender, rounded or conical head with no beak; melon overhangs tip of lower jaw (adult male only); unique 'elbow' on flippers; prominent, falcate fin; fairly acrobatic.

DIET
Mostly fish and squid, known to attack other cetaceans.

BREEDING
Calving interval possibly up to 7 years; gestation 14–16 months.

The false killer whale can look rather menacing and has been known to attack groups of small cetaceans. On one occasion it even attacked a nursery school of sperm whales and, on another, killed a humpback whale calf. Yet it is often seen in the company of bottlenose dolphins and, in captivity, shows less aggression than its smaller relative the pygmy killer whale. One of the largest members of the dolphin family, in many ways it behaves more like an oceanic dolphin: it leaps high into the air, makes rapid turns underwater, and even rides the bow-waves of boats and ships. It is a fast and active swimmer, often lifting its entire head and much of its body out of the water when it surfaces. False killer whales seem to be susceptible to stranding, and sometimes come ashore in huge numbers (more than 800 in one exceptional case). They normally occur in groups of around 20 animals, but it is not unusual for many smaller groups to travel together. They are unpopular with fishermen and have a reputation for

stealing fish such as tuna from baited lines. The common name refers to a similarity in skull morphology with the killer whale, rather than a similarity in external appearance.

Where to look

Widely distributed in tropical, sub-tropical and warm temperate waters worldwide (including enclosed seas such as the Mediterranean and Red Sea). False killer whales prefer deep water and, except around oceanic islands, are normally encountered offshore. Small numbers drown in fishing nets and are hunted for food or by fishermen who regard them as competitors. A few are also captured for marine parks.

Long-finned Pilot Whale
Globicephala melas

ID FACT FILE

Other names
Caaing whale, blackfish, pothead whale.

Maximum length
6.3 metres (male), 4.8 metres (female).

Maximum weight
Possibly 3 tonnes.

Field ID
Long, stocky body; black, grey or dark brown; pale saddle-patch behind fin; large, rounded head with bulbous melon; light diagonal stripe behind each eye (mainly southern hemisphere); no visible beak; exceptionally long flippers; low, broad-based fin far forward on body (sweeps backward).

Diet
Mainly squid and fish, some crustaceans.

Breeding
Calves every 3–5 years; gestation 12 months.

Long-finned and short-finned pilot whales are almost impossible to tell apart at sea but, fortunately, there is relatively little overlap in their range. The main differences are subtle: in the length of the flippers (proportionally longer in long-finned), the shape of the skull (slightly longer and narrower in long-finned) and the number of teeth (a few more in long-finned). There are also significant differences between the vocalisations of the two species: the calls of long-finned pilot whales are of a lower frequency and a narrower frequency range than those of short-finned pilot whales. There are two recognised sub-species of long-finned pilot whale: one in the northern hemisphere and the other thousands of kilometres away in the southern hemisphere. They strand more frequently than many other species and are often involved in mass strandings involving hundreds of animals. Limited estimates of abundance suggest a population of about three-quarters of a million in the central and eastern North Atlantic, at least 10,000 in the western North Atlantic and some 200,000 in the Southern Ocean.

Where to look
The long-finned pilot whale has two distinct populations: one in the cool, deep temperate waters of the North Atlantic (including the western Mediterranean Sea) and the other throughout the Southern Ocean. These two populations are completely isolated. There is some overlap in range with the short-finned pilot whale. More than 1,000 long-finned pilot whales are killed every year in the Faroe Islands, and smaller numbers in other parts of the world.

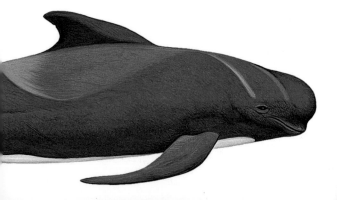

Short-finned Pilot Whale

Globicephala macrorhynchus

ID FACT FILE

OTHER NAMES
Pacific pilot whale, blackfish, pothead whale.

MAXIMUM LENGTH
7.2 metres (male), 5.1 metres (female).

MAXIMUM WEIGHT
Possibly 4 tonnes.

FIELD ID
Long, stocky body; black, grey or dark brown; pale saddle-patch behind fin (variable); large, rounded head with bulbous melon; may be light diagonal stripe behind each eye; no visible beak; shorter flippers than long-finned; low, broad-based fin far forward on body (sweeps backward).

DIET
Mainly squid, some fish and octopuses.

BREEDING
Calves every 5–8 years; gestation 15-16 months.

Pilot whales are among the largest members of the dolphin family. Their name originates from an early theory (probably not true) that a school is piloted or led by one particular leader. Both long-finned and short-finned pilot whales exhibit striking sexual dimorphism in size: males are considerably longer than females and have a more pronounced melon and much larger dorsal fin. They are highly social animals, typically living in small groups (10–20 individuals in long-finned and 15–90 in short-finned), which often come together to form much larger gatherings. As in killer whale pods, these close-knit families stay together for life and most individuals never leave (although males mate with females from other groups to avoid inbreeding). Females continue to ovulate until their late thirties and may still be lactating in their late forties; they probably live well into their sixties. Limited estimates of abundance suggest a population of some 160,000 in the eastern tropical Pacific and 30,000–50,000 in southern Japan. Several hundred short-finned pilot whales are killed annually in Japan and the Caribbean, and they are hunted in Indonesia and Sri Lanka.

SHORT-FINNED PILOT WHALE

Where to look
The short-finned pilot whale prefers warm water
and is found worldwide in the tropics and sub-
tropics and in warm temperate regions. It is
common in the Canary Islands and occurs around
Madeira and the Azores, but is absent from the
Mediterranean. There is little, but probably some,
overlap in range with the long-finned pilot whale –
mainly in temperate waters of the Atlantic, in the
Pacific off the coast of Peru, Tasmania and the
south-east coast of Australia, and off South Africa.

Killer Whale

Orcinus orca

ID FACT FILE

OTHER NAMES
Orca, blackfish.

MAXIMUM LENGTH
9 metres (male),
7.7 metres
(female).

MAXIMUM WEIGHT
Possibly 9 tonnes
(heaviest on
record 5.6
tonnes).

FIELD ID
Large, stocky
body; jet-black
and brilliant
white coloration;
white patch
behind each eye;
extremely tall,
black triangular
fin of male
(smaller and
falcate in
females and
calves); grey
saddle-patch
behind fin; large,
paddle-shaped
flippers.

DIET
Extremely varied,
from squid and
fish to birds and
marine mammals
(each pod tends
to specialise).

BREEDING
Calving interval
averages 5
years; gestation
15–18 months.

When Basque whalers saw killer whales feeding on the carcasses of dead whales, they called them 'whale killers' and the name stuck. But many people prefer to use the more politically correct name, orca, to avoid any negative connotations. Unfortunately, though, the Latin *orcus* means 'belonging to the kingdom of the dead'. Killer whales have been studied in the wild for more than 30 years. Several distinct forms are known – dubbed residents, transients and offshores – which differ significantly in appearance, behaviour, group size and diet. Another form living in the Antarctic has been proposed as a separate species, but this is controversial. Studies on resident whales living in the eastern North Pacific show that the basic social unit is the matrilineal group, which consists of up to four generations (a female, her sons and daughters, and the offspring of her daughters); they are all closely related and usually stay together for life. Several matrilineal groups together form an extended family called a pod; and several pods, which share similar dialects, are called a clan. Most killer whale populations are numbered in the hundreds or low thousands, but there may be 70,000–80,000 in the Antarctic.

KILLER WHALE

male

Where to look

Despite its rather patchy distribution, the killer whale is one of the most wide-ranging mammals on Earth. It occurs in all seas and oceans, from the equator to the high Arctic and the Antarctic pack ice and from near the coast to far offshore. However, it generally prefers cooler inshore waters. It is still persecuted by some fishermen and periodically caught for public display in aquaria.

Tucuxi
Sotalia fluviatilis

ID FACT FILE

OTHER NAMES
Estuarine
dolphin.
MAXIMUM LENGTH
2.1 metres
(marine), 1.5
metres
(freshwater).
MAXIMUM WEIGHT
45 kilograms.
FIELD ID
Small, robust
body; grey
upperside, light
underside
(sometimes
appears pink –
especially on the
sides and
underside);
prominent, fairly
slender beak;
slightly rounded
melon; roughly
triangular fin (low
in profile).
DIET
Mainly fish,
some
crustaceans.
BREEDING
Calving interval
unknown;
gestation
probably 10
months.

There are two sub-species of tucuxi
(pronounced tookooshee): a relatively
small one found in lakes and rivers, and a
considerably larger one in the sea. The
riverine form has been studied in some
detail, but less is
known about the
marine form.

Despite its large riverine population, it is
a member of the family Delphinidae and
is not closely related to the 'true' river
dolphins (although, in the Amazon Basin,
it is not unusual to see tucuxis feeding in
the company of Amazon river dolphins).
It is often referred to simply as 'Sotalia',
which is the first part of its scientific
name. At first glance it looks rather like a
small bottlenose dolphin – and
sometimes behaves like one, too. Tucuxis
are fairly active at the surface and can be
seen breaching, spyhopping and
splashing; they are not known to bow-
ride, but will sometimes play in the wake
of passing boats and ships. As well as

hunting, incidental capture in fishing nets and
conflicts with fisheries, the damming of the Amazon,
mangrove degradation and coastal pollution are all
threats.

Where to look
The tucuxi is found in warm, shallow coastal waters
of north-eastern South America and eastern Central
America (from Nicaragua to Florianópolis in Brazil)
and throughout much of the Amazon River basin.
Coastal populations are most common in estuaries
and large bays, while riverine ones are found as far
as 2,500 kilometres up the Amazon. They appear to
be fairly common over much of their range.

Spinner Dolphin
Stenella longirostris

ID FACT FILE

OTHER NAMES
Long-snouted
spinner,
longsnout,
rollover, long-
beaked dolphin.

MAXIMUM LENGTH
2.4 metres.

MAXIMUM WEIGHT
90 kilograms.

FIELD ID
Slender body;
three-part colour
pattern; long,
narrow beak with
dark tip; upper
jaw grey, lower
jaw often cream;
dark stripe from
eye to flipper;
gently-sloping
melon; tall fin can
be slightly falcate
or erect (leans
forward in some
individuals);
performs high,
spinning leaps.

DIET
Fish, squid and
crustaceans.

BREEDING
Calves every 3
years; gestation
just over 10
months.

One of the most acrobatic of all dolphins, the spinner was named for its incredibly high spinning leaps. It can spin round on its longitudinal axis as many as seven times before splashing back into the water. No other cetacean shows so much variation in appearance from one region to another and there are currently four recognised sub-species, differing greatly in body shape, size, colour and even behaviour. The colour pattern in most regions is basically three-part, albeit with considerable regional differences, consisting of a dark-grey cape, light-grey sides and white underside. Numbers were reduced significantly by tuna fishing in the eastern tropical Pacific (which has been responsible for killing more dolphins in the past 35 years than any other human activity). Fortunately, public outrage has forced the authorities to introduce new rules and regulations, which include releasing dolphins from the nets when they are captured, and the scale of the slaughter has dropped to thousands (rather than hundreds of

thousands) of deaths a year. However, the
population of eastern spinners is still probably
less than half its original size.

Where to look

The spinner is found mainly in tropical and sub-
tropical waters worldwide, although it sometimes
occurs in warm temperate waters as well.
Depending on the sub-species, it can be seen in
shallow water close to shore, around oceanic islands
or far out to sea. Many spinners are hunted or
drowned in gill nets every year, especially in
Australia and Asia. Despite all the threats, it is still
fairly common in some parts of its range.

Clymene Dolphin

Stenella clymene

ID FACT FILE

OTHER NAMES
Short-snouted
spinner dolphin,
Senegal dolphin,
helmet dolphin.

MAXIMUM LENGTH
2 metres.

MAXIMUM WEIGHT
80 kilograms.

FIELD ID
Relatively small,
fairly robust
body; three-toned
colour pattern;
dark grey or
black cape dips
below fin; long
beak with black
tip, lips and
'moustache';
pale grey stripe
from eye to
flipper; dark,
slender flippers;
prominent,
slightly falcate or
triangular fin.

DIET
Fish and squid.

BREEDING
Calving interval
and gestation
period unknown.

For many years the clymene dolphin, or short-snouted spinner dolphin as it is often called, was considered to be one of the many variations of the long-snouted spinner. The two animals sometimes associate with one another and, like the spinner, the clymene has a three-toned colouration: a dark grey cape, lighter grey sides, and a white underside. Some populations even spin longitudinally when breaching, although not as frequently or as elaborately as spinners. But the clymene dolphin (pronounced cly-mee-nee) was officially classified as a separate species in 1981. There is considerable overlap in range between the two species in the Atlantic, and they can be difficult to tell apart at sea. The clymene dolphin is usually seen in groups of up to 50 animals (although

several hundred have been observed together).
Schools may be segregated by sex, and possibly
age, since several mass strandings have consisted
almost entirely of females or males. It is a keen
bow-rider and will go out of its way to accompany
a boat or ship, yet remains one of the least-known
oceanic dolphins.

Where to look
Found in warm temperate, sub-tropical and tropical
waters of the Atlantic Ocean, the clymene dolphin
occurs mainly in deep waters offshore. It appears
to be absent from the Mediterranean, but details
of its distribution are lacking. Little is also known
about its abundance. Some hunting takes place
in the Caribbean and it is caught incidentally in
fishing nets in many parts of its range, especially
in West Africa.

Striped Dolphin
Stenella coeruleoalba

ID FACT FILE

OTHER NAMES
Streaker,
whitebelly.

MAXIMUM LENGTH
2.7 metres.

MAXIMUM WEIGHT
160 kilograms.

FIELD ID
Fairly robust
body; bluish-grey
upperside, pale
grey sides and
tail stock, white
or pinkish
underside; long,
dark side stripe;
pale shoulder
blaze sweeping
up towards fin;
dark stripe from
eye to flipper;
prominent beak;
dark, prominent
fin.

DIET
Squid and fish
(lanternfish a
favourite in some
areas).

BREEDING
Calves every 4
years; gestation
12–13 months.

Striped dolphins are highly conspicuous animals, seeming to spend an inordinate amount of their time in the air. Their acrobatic repertoire includes high breaches, belly-flops, chin-slaps, back somersaults, tail spins, and upside-down porpoising. They also have a unique behaviour, called 'roto-tailing', which involves leaping into a high arc and then rapidly rotating the tail before re-entering the water. Their distinctive stripes, and the speed at which they swim, prompted fishermen to call them 'streakers'. In some parts of the world they readily approach boats, but they are more wary and do not bow-ride in the eastern tropical Pacific where, until quite recently, considerable numbers were killed by the tuna-fishing industry. Known to live to the ripe old age of nearly 60 years, they are fairly well known and several different populations have been studied in detail.

Where to look

Found worldwide, striped dolphins live mainly in
tropical, sub-tropical and warm temperate waters –
although they occur as far north as southern
Greenland and Iceland. Despite large numbers
being killed incidentally by a pelagic drift-net
fishery, they are probably the commonest cetaceans
in the Mediterranean Sea. Usually encountered
offshore, they are hunted in some regions of the
world, especially in the Japanese drive fishery.

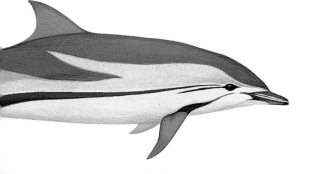

Pantropical Spotted Dolphin
Stenella attenuata

Tuna-fishing operations in the eastern tropical Pacific killed so many pantropical spotted dolphins in the 1960s, 1970s and 1980s that the regional population declined by as much as 75 per cent. Literally millions of the animals were killed, along with huge numbers of other dolphin species. New laws and release techniques have reduced the level of the slaughter dramatically, but it has still not been stopped altogether. It is still unclear why the dolphins associate with tuna – it might increase foraging efficiency or provide better protection from predators. Adults are usually covered in white spots, which fuse and fade to a medium-grey as they get older, but newborn calves are unspotted. However, there is a lot of variation in the appearance of individuals within a population and between populations in different parts of the world. Three sub-species are currently recognised: one living mainly in coastal waters of the

eastern Pacific tends to be larger, more spotted and more robust. Pantropical spotted dolphins spend a lot of time in the air and youngsters, in particular, can make some impressively high vertical leaps.

Where to look
Found worldwide in tropical and some sub-tropical waters of the Atlantic, Pacific and Indian Oceans, the pantropical spotted dolphin occurs both inshore and offshore. It is most abundant nearer the equator, but is known as far north as 40°N and as far south as 40°S. Although hunted in many parts of the world and caught incidentally in fishing nets, it is still surprisingly abundant and the world population is estimated to be at least three million.

Atlantic Spotted Dolphin

Stenella frontalis

ID FACT FILE

OTHER NAMES
Spotter, bridled
dolphin, Gulf
Stream spotted
dolphin.
MAXIMUM LENGTH
2.3 metres.
MAXIMUM WEIGHT
140 kilograms.
FIELD ID
Fairly robust
head and body;
three-toned
colour pattern
(not always
clear); most
adults heavily
spotted; pale
diagonal
shoulder blaze
sweeping up
towards fin;
chunky, white-
tipped beak;
tall, falcate fin;
variable
appearance
within herd.
DIET
Squid and fish,
some benthic
invertebrates.
BREEDING
Calves every 3–4
years; gestation
period unknown.

There are so many variations in the
markings of spotted dolphins
that their taxonomy has
puzzled experts for a
long time. But
the Atlantic
spotted dolphin is one of just two
currently recognised species. Most adults
have dark spots on the underside and
light spots on the sides and back, but
some are not spotted at all and others are
so heavily spotted they appear almost
white from a distance. Young animals
have no spots but these begin to appear
as they grow older. The Atlantic spotted
dolphin is difficult to tell apart from the
very similar pantropical spotted dolphin,
but the distinctive diagonal shoulder
blaze that sweeps up through the cape
towards the dorsal fin is diagnostic. One
particular population of Atlantic spotted
dolphins on Little Bahama Bank, north
of the Bahamas, has been studied in
great detail since the 1970s, but the
species is less well known elsewhere in
the Atlantic.

Where to look

As its name suggests, the Atlantic spotted
dolphin is found in the Atlantic – both
North and South – in warm temperate,
sub-tropical and tropical waters. The
range extends from about 50°N to 25°S,
but it does not appear to include the

Mediterranean Sea. Most information is from coastal areas, but sightings are also fairly common far from land. It is hunted in some areas and killed incidentally in fisheries in the Caribbean and West Africa.

Atlantic Hump-backed Dolphin

Sousa teuszii

ID FACT FILE

OTHER NAMES
Cameroon
dolphin.

MAXIMUM LENGTH
2.8 metres.

MAXIMUM WEIGHT
260 kilograms.

FIELD ID
Robust body;
slate-grey
upperside and
sides, paler
underside;
elongated hump
on back; small
fin sits on hump;
long, slender
beak; beak
exposed on
surfacing; back
strongly arched
on diving; flukes
often raised on
diving.

DIET
Fish, squid and
octopuses.

BREEDING
Calves every 3
years; gestation
10–12 months.

Once incorrectly believed to be the only plant-eating dolphin, the Atlantic hump-backed dolphin is a strange-looking animal with a conspicuous, elongated hump on its back. The dorsal fin sits on top of the hump, giving it a rather top-heavy appearance. There appears to be no overlap in range with the Indo-Pacific hump-backed dolphin, which just enters the Atlantic at the southern tip of Africa, but recent morphological studies and genetic analyses suggest that it may belong to the same species. Atlantic hump-backed dolphins are well known for joining bottlenose dolphins in cooperating with Mauritanian fishermen around Cap Timiris, north of Nouakchott, by driving fish towards their nets. However, they are threatened throughout their range by entanglement in fishing nets and, in some areas, by hunting. Living very close to shore, in water typically less than 25 metres deep, they are also vulnerable to threats such as habitat destruction and disturbance.

Where to look

There is little information on the precise range of Atlantic hump-backed dolphins, but they are known from the coastal waters of tropical and sub-tropical West Africa (southern Morocco to Cameroon and possibly as far south as Angola). They certainly appear to have a considerably smaller range than their Indo-Pacific relatives. They are most common around estuaries and mangrove swamps and are known to enter the Niger and some other rivers (though they usually remain within the tidal zone).

Indo-Pacific Hump-backed Dolphin

Sousa chinensis

OTHER NAMES
Chinese white
dolphin, pink
dolphin.
MAXIMUM LENGTH
2.8 metres.
MAXIMUM WEIGHT
260 kilograms.
FIELD ID
Robust body;
grey, brown, pink,
white or mottled
colour; elongated
hump on back
(animals west of
Sumatra only);
small fin sits on
hump; long,
slender beak;
beak exposed on
surfacing; back
strongly arched
on diving; flukes
often raised on
diving.
DIET
Fish, squid and
octopuses.
BREEDING
Calves every 3
years; gestation
10–12 months.

Indo-Pacific hump-backed dolphins vary greatly in appearance, depending on where they live. The animals west of Sumatra, in Indonesia, have a fatty hump on their backs and a relatively small dorsal fin on top, whereas those living east and south of Sumatra have a less pronounced hump (or no hump at all) but a more prominent dorsal fin. There are also several distinct colour variations, including pure white, grey, and even pink. There is an interesting population in the South China Sea, commonly known as Chinese white dolphins, which are white or bright pink in colour. Inevitably, the classification of hump-backed dolphins is still under discussion. Some evidence suggests that there should be just one species (*Sousa chinensis*), but other evidence supports the case for three species: Pacific hump-backed (*Sousa chinensis*), Atlantic hump-backed (*Sousa teuszii*) and a third in the Indian Ocean called the Indian hump-backed (*Sousa plumbea*). The hump

occurs only in the *teuszii* and *plumbea* forms. They
are vulnerable living close to shore and threatened
by hunting in some areas as well as entanglement in
fishing nets and anti-shark nets.

Where to look
Indo-Pacific hump-backed dolphins are found in
shallow coastal waters in the tropics and sub-tropics,
from northern Australia and southern China in the
east, around the Indian Ocean, to southern Africa in
the west. They rarely enter water more than 25
metres deep and are seldom seen more than a few
kilometres from shore. They sometimes enter rivers,
though rarely more than a few kilometres upstream
and usually within the tidal zone.

Northern Rightwhale Dolphin

Lissodelphis borealis

ID FACT FILE

OTHER NAMES
Pacific rightwhale
porpoise.

MAXIMUM LENGTH
3.1 metres.

MAXIMUM WEIGHT
115 kilograms.

FIELD ID
Streamlined,
slender body;
predominantly
black with white
underside; no
fin; white spot
under short,
slender beak;
predominantly
black flippers;
low-angled leaps
give impression
of bouncy
swimming
motion.

DIET
Fish (especially
lanternfish) and
squid.

BREEDING
Calves every 2
years; gestation
12–13 months.

Superficially similar in appearance to its southern counterpart, the northern rightwhale dolphin is the only dolphin in the North Pacific without a dorsal fin. Its striking black-and-white body pattern is also distinctive, though in the water it often appears to be entirely black. The calves of both species are usually dark grey or brown – they become black-and-white like their parents when they are about a year old. Northern rightwhale

dolphins are capable of swimming very fast, making long, low-angled leaps and appearing to bounce across the water, but they sometimes surface slowly and keep a low profile – making them difficult to see in anything but the calmest conditions. They are often encountered in the company of other cetaceans, especially

Pacific white-sided dolphins, and travel in huge schools of up to 3,000 animals. Tens of thousands were killed in the 1980s in drift nets set for squid (which are now banned on the high seas). Relatively small numbers are taken by Japan's harpoon fishery and others are drowned in nets on both sides of the Pacific, especially in the Japanese and Russian purse-seine fisheries.

Where to look
Northern rightwhale dolphins are found in cool temperate and sub-Arctic waters across the northern North Pacific, mainly in deep, offshore waters between 34°N and 55°N (34°N and 47°N in mid-ocean). More southerly records normally occur where the water temperature is unusually low. They are rarely seen near land, except in sufficiently deep water. There is no overlap in range with the southern rightwhale dolphin – the two species are separated by many thousands of kilometres.

Southern Rightwhale Dolphin

Lissodelphis peronii

ID FACT FILE

OTHER NAMES
Mealy-mouthed porpoise.

MAXIMUM LENGTH
3 metres.

MAXIMUM WEIGHT
120 kilograms.

FIELD ID
Streamlined, slender body; stark black-and-white colour pattern (jet-black upperside, white underside); no fin; short, white beak; predominantly white flippers; low-angled leaps give impression of bouncy swimming motion.

DIET
Fish (especially lanternfish) and squid.

BREEDING
Calving interval and gestation period unknown.

The only dolphin in the southern hemisphere without a dorsal fin, the southern rightwhale dolphin is very distinctive with its striking black-and-white body pattern. Despite its remote offshore distribution, it is fairly easy to see in the right areas and will sometimes even bow-ride. From a distance, schools of fast-swimming southern rightwhale

dolphins look remarkably similar to penguins; and, when swimming slowly, they can be mistaken for porpoising fur seals or sea lions. Slow-swimming gives them a very low profile and makes them difficult to see in anything but the calmest conditions. They travel in large schools of up to 1,000 animals and often associate with long-finned pilot whales or dusky dolphins. They are killed for human consumption or crab bait off Chile and Peru, and increasing numbers drown in fishing nets in the rapidly-developing swordfish gill-net fishery off Chile. Both northern and southern rightwhale dolphins were named after the much larger right whales, which also lack dorsal fins.

Where to look

Found mainly between the Tropic of Capricorn and the Antarctic Convergence, southern rightwhale dolphins live in the cold temperate to sub-Antarctic waters of the southern hemisphere. They occur further north in some parts of their range, especially where cold currents such as the Humboldt and Benguela push into sub-tropical latitudes. Rarely seen near land, they prefer deep water.

Short-beaked Common Dolphin

Delphinus delphis

ID FACT FILE

OTHER NAMES
Criss-cross
dolphin,
saddleback
dolphin, white-
bellied porpoise,
common
porpoise.
MAXIMUM LENGTH
2.7 metres.
MAXIMUM WEIGHT
150 kilograms.
FIELD ID
Slightly robust
body; criss-cross
pattern on sides;
dark cape with
'V' directly under
fin; yellow tan
patch on sides,
white underside,
pale grey tail
stock; dark line
from flipper to
beak; prominent
beak; tall,
moderately
falcate fin; crisp
colour pattern.
DIET
Fish and squid.
BREEDING
Calves every 1–3
years; gestation
10–11 months.

There are many different forms of
common dolphin around the world and
numerous species have been proposed
over the years. They all have the
distinctive hourglass pattern of white,
grey, yellow and black on their sides, but
show many differences within this basic
framework. In 1995, though, the
common dolphin was officially separated
into two distinct species, now known as
the short-beaked common dolphin and
the long-beaked common dolphin. These
show many subtle genetic, physical and
behavioural differences although, at sea,
they can still be very difficult to tell apart.
In general terms, the short-beaked is a
little more robust, with a slightly shorter
beak and crisper colour pattern. There
are also subtle differences in the facial
pattern. Huge numbers of short-beaked
common dolphins were killed by Turkish
and Russian fishermen in the Black Sea,
severely depleting the population there
by the time hunting ceased in the 1980s.
Significant numbers are drowned in
fishing nets across their range, and local
populations seem to be declining in
some areas.

Where to look

The short-beaked common dolphin is the most
numerous dolphin in offshore warm temperate,
sub-tropical and tropical waters of the Atlantic and
Pacific Oceans. It is especially common in deep
water along the shelf edge and over seamounts and
submarine canyons, but sometimes occurs in
shallower water close to shore. It occurs in both the
Mediterranean and Black Seas.

Long-beaked Common Dolphin

Delphinus capensis

ID FACT FILE

OTHER NAMES
Criss-cross
dolphin,
saddleback
dolphin, white-
bellied porpoise,
common
porpoise.

MAXIMUM LENGTH
2.5 metres.

MAXIMUM WEIGHT
150 kilograms.

FIELD ID
Slender body;
criss-cross
pattern on sides;
dark cape with
'v' under fin;
yellowy tan patch
on sides, white
underside, pale
grey tail stock;
dark line from
flipper to beak;
prominent beak;
tall, moderately
falcate fin;
muted colour
pattern.

DIET
Fish and squid.

BREEDING
Probably calves
every 2–3 years;
gestation about
10–11 months.

The long-beaked common dolphin is not as well known as its short-beaked relative. This is partly because it is not as common but also because, until quite recently, it was considered merely as a type of short-beaked common dolphin rather than a separate species in its own right. Now the taxonomists are puzzling over a possible third species, found in the Red Sea, the northern Indian Ocean and south-east Asia, which has a similarly long beak but differs in other ways. It has tentatively been named *Delphinus tropicalis* – but its taxonomic status is still uncertain and, in the meantime, it is regarded as a regional variant of the long-beaked. It is not unusual to see schools of long-beaked and short-beaked common dolphins in the same general area on the same day, especially in coastal waters. However, long-beaked seem to prefer shallower and warmer water and usually occur closer to shore. All common dolphins can be distinguished from other dolphins by the unique criss-cross colour pattern on their sides.

LONG-BEAKED COMMON DOLPHIN

Where to look

Unlike the short-beaked common dolphin, the
long-beaked is usually found close to shore. It lives
in warm temperate, sub-tropical and tropical
waters of the Pacific, Atlantic and Indian Oceans.
However, information is fairly limited, because
the earlier confusion with short-beaked common
dolphins means that many distribution records
have not separated the two species. The long-
beaked common dolphin is hunted in Peru and
possibly elsewhere.

Rough-toothed Dolphin
Steno bredanensis

ID FACT FILE

OTHER NAMES
Slopehead.
MAXIMUM LENGTH
2.7 metres.
MAXIMUM WEIGHT
160 kilograms.
FIELD ID
Slightly robust body; dark, narrow cape; dark and pinkish-white blotches; tall, falcate fin; conical head; long, narrow beak continuous with forehead; white or pinkish-white lips and throat; tip of beak sometimes white; dark patch around eyes.
DIET
Fish, squid and octopuses.
BREEDING
Calving interval and gestation period unknown.

A strange-looking dolphin, with a slightly reptilian appearance, the rough-toothed dolphin is named for a series of fine, vertical wrinkles on the enamel cap of each tooth. Its uniquely-sloping forehead, which lacks a crease at the base of the beak, makes it quite easy to identify at close range. Many individuals have quite distinctive light-coloured blotches, which may be caused by the bites of large squid or cookie-cutter sharks. Rough-toothed dolphins are usually seen in small groups of 10–20 animals, although occasionally there may be as many as 50 travelling together (and one exceptional observation in Hawaii recorded more than 300). They are fairly slow swimmers, but have been known to ride bow waves and perform various aerial behaviours. Often seen in the company of other dolphins, in the eastern tropical Pacific they also associate with flotsam. They have been hunted in many parts of their range, especially in Asia and West Africa, and are almost certainly caught incidentally in fishing nets.

Where to look
Found worldwide in deep oceanic waters of the
tropics, sub-tropics and some warm temperate
regions, the rough-toothed dolphin rarely occurs
close to shore except around oceanic islands or
where the continental shelf is narrow (although it is
frequently encountered in shallow coastal waters in
Brazil). With the notable exception of the Maldives,
there are relatively few records from the poorly-
studied Indian Ocean.

Risso's Dolphin
Grampus griseus

Risso's dolphins are unmistakable, with their slightly bulging foreheads, remarkably tall dorsal fins and distinctive battered appearance. The scratches and scars on their bodies are caused mainly by the teeth of other Risso's dolphins, although confrontations with squid may also be to blame. The dorsal fin and flippers always remain dark but their

RISSO'S DOLPHIN

body colour tends to lighten with age: young animals are mainly grey or brown at birth, then darken to nearly black before lightening as they mature. The huge variation in colour between individuals within a school – from almost as white as belugas to nearly as dark as pilot whales – is a distinctive feature of Risso's dolphins. Another unique feature, albeit only visible at close range, is a vertical crease down the centre of the forehead. Risso's dolphins are usually seen in groups of up to 50 individuals (the average number is 25) but temporary aggregations of hundreds or even several thousand are seen occasionally. They are named after the person who described the type specimen to Georges Cuvier, who formally described the species in 1812.

Where to look
Found worldwide in deep tropical to warm temperate waters, including enclosed seas such as the Mediterranean and Red Sea, Risso's dolphins seem to prefer the steepest edges along the continental shelf. Some individuals may move to higher latitudes during the summer. They are hunted in Sri Lanka, Japan, Indonesia, the Solomon Islands and the Lesser Antilles and are caught incidentally in a wide variety of fishing gear. However, they still seem to be fairly common over much of their range.

Irrawaddy Dolphin

Orcaella brevirostris

ID FACT FILE

OTHER NAMES
Snubfin dolphin.

MAXIMUM LENGTH
2.8 metres.

MAXIMUM WEIGHT
130 kilograms.

FIELD ID
Slender body; light-grey coloured upperside and sides, slightly lighter underside; large melon; rounded head with no beak; small, stubby (often triangular) fin; large, spatulate flippers.

DIET
Mainly fish, some squid, octopuses, cuttlefish and crustaceans.

BREEDING
Calving interval unknown; gestation about 14 months.

A rather unusual dolphin, resembling a small beluga with a dorsal fin, the Irrawaddy dolphin has a strange habit of spitting water from its mouth while spyhopping. Usually quiet and undemonstrative, it tends to be difficult to find in turbid conditions but can sometimes be located by its loud blow. The population off north-eastern Australia and Papua New Guinea is unlike other populations, with a lighter, three-toned colour pattern, and genetic studies may ultimately prove it to be a separate species (tentatively called the Australian snubfin dolphin, *Orcaella heinsohni*). The Irrawaddy dolphin is revered as a reincarnated human in Laos and Cambodia and some individuals in the Irrawaddy and Mekong Rivers cooperate with local fishermen by driving fish into their nets. But elsewhere they are drowned in a variety of

fishing nets and anti-shark nets, killed by explosive
fishing methods, hunted and captured alive for
oceanaria. Their riverine and coastal habitat is also
vulnerable to human disturbance, damming,
pollution and industrial development. Consequently,
the Irrawaddy dolphin is believed to be disappearing
from much of its range. It is named after the large
river in Myanmar (formerly Burma).

Where to look
Found in major river systems and shallow coastal
waters (especially mangrove swamps), the Irrawaddy
dolphin lives in
the tropical Indo-
Pacific (from the
western Bay of Bengal to
northern Australia). There are populations in
the Brahmaputra and Ganges, India; Mekong,
Vietnam, Laos and Cambodia; Mahakam, Borneo;
and Irrawaddy, Myanmar (as far as 1,300 kilometres
upstream). It is rarely more than a few kilometres
from shore. Some individuals probably spend all
their lives in freshwater.

Fraser's Dolphin
Lagenodelphis hosei

ID FACT FILE

OTHER NAMES
White-bellied
dolphin, Sarawak
dolphin,
shortsnout
dolphin, Bornean
dolphin.

MAXIMUM LENGTH
2.7 metres.

MAXIMUM WEIGHT
210 kilograms.

FIELD ID
Stocky body;
blue-grey or grey-
brown cape, light
grey sides,
creamy-white or
pinkish-white
underside; dark
lateral stripe;
dark stripe from
beak, across
eyes, to flippers;
small, triangular
or slightly falcate
fin; short but
well-defined
beak; tiny
flippers.

DIET
Fish, squid and
crustaceans.

BREEDING
Calves every 2
years; gestation
about 12–13
months.

Until the early 1970s, Fraser's dolphin had not been seen alive. But it has been observed many times since and is regularly encountered on dolphin watching tours in the Caribbean, the Maldives and elsewhere. It certainly does not seem to be as rare as was once thought. Officially named from a single skull found in 1895 on a beach in Sarawak, on the island of Borneo, it was originally known as the Sarawak dolphin. It was named after the British scientist Francis Fraser, who formally described the species in 1956. The distinctive dark stripes and bandit-like face mask are not always present, and vary greatly with age and sex, but at least some individuals in a school of Fraser's dolphins are usually easy to recognise. They tend to live in large schools (typically 100 to 500 but, in some parts of their range, as many as 1,000) and are sometimes seen in the company of melon-headed, false killer and short-finned pilot whales and several dolphin species.

Where to look

Fraser's dolphin is found worldwide in deep tropical
and warm temperate waters, mainly between about
30°N and 30°S. It is rarely seen inshore, except
around oceanic islands and in areas with a narrow
continental shelf. Significant numbers probably
drown in a variety of fishing nets, and relatively
small numbers are killed by harpoon and drive
fisheries in Asia and elsewhere. A stranding in
Brittany, France, was probably a vagrant school.

Common Bottlenose Dolphin

Tursiops truncatus

ID FACT FILE

OTHER NAMES
Bottle-nosed
dolphin, Atlantic
bottlenose
dolphin.
MAXIMUM LENGTH
3.8 metres.
MAXIMUM WEIGHT
600 kilograms.
FIELD ID
Robust head and
body; subdued
grey or blue-grey
colouring with
darker cape
(indistinct in
many lighting
conditions);
prominent,
falcate fin;
distinct, stubby
beak with
marked melon
crease; rounded
melon.
DIET
Fish, squid,
crustaceans and
wide variety of
other prey.
BREEDING
Calves every 3–6
years; gestation
12 months.

The bottlenose dolphin is the archetypal dolphin. It figured prominently in ancient Greek and Roman mythology and, more recently, has been the star of television programmes, films and marine parks around the world. It is probably the species most people imagine when the word 'dolphin' is mentioned and is one of the most-studied and best-known of all the cetaceans. There are many variations, differing considerably in size, shape and colour. In particular, there is a smaller, lighter inshore form and a larger, more robust offshore form. Inshore animals tend to live in smaller groups of up to 15 individuals, while it is not unusual to see groups of several hundred offshore animals. Wild bottlenose dolphins (usually males) sometimes become 'friendlies' and seem more interested in sharing the company of human swimmers and small boats than of other dolphins. They also seem to like the company of other cetaceans, particularly pilot whales, although can be quite aggressive towards other species: in the Moray Firth, Scotland, they are known to kill harbour porpoises.

Where to look

Common bottlenose dolphins live in tropical to temperate waters worldwide, close to shore and far out to sea. They are found in many enclosed seas, including the Black and Mediterranean Seas

(although the Black Sea population was severely depleted by a fishery which is now banned). There is considerable overlap in range with the Indo-Pacific bottlenose dolphin. Hunting in some areas, such as Japan, Sri Lanka, the Philippines and Chile, may be a threat to local populations.

Indo-Pacific Bottlenose Dolphin

Tursiops aduncus

ID FACT FILE

OTHER NAMES
Bottle-nosed
dolphin, Pacific
bottlenose
dolphin, Indian
Ocean
bottlenose
dolphin.

MAXIMUM LENGTH
2.6 metres.

MAXIMUM WEIGHT
230 kilograms.

FIELD ID
Slender head and
body; subdued
grey or blue-grey
colouring with
darker cape
(indistinct in
many lighting
conditions); dark
spots on
underside and
sides (absent in
some
individuals);
prominent,
falcate fin;
slender beak
with melon
crease.

DIET
Fish and squid,
some
crustaceans and
other prey.

BREEDING
Calves every 4–6
years; gestation
12 months.

The possibility of a separate species of
bottlenose dolphin, living in the Pacific
and Indian Oceans, has been discussed
for many years. With the help of genetic
research the Indo-Pacific bottlenose
dolphin was finally given separate species
status in the late 1990s, but the major
differences between the two have yet to
be fully analysed and described. The
Indo-Pacific bottlenose tends to be
considerably smaller and less robust, with
a longer, more slender beak and
proportionally larger dorsal fin and
flippers; it also develops dark spots on
the underside and sides when it is
sexually mature (although spotting is
variable between populations and absent
from some individuals). The differences
between the two species are so

significant, despite superficial similarities in their
appearance, that the Indo-Pacific bottlenose dolphin
may be more closely related to spotted, striped and
spinner dolphins than to its namesake. In some parts
of the world it is found in mixed schools with
common bottlenose dolphins and other dolphin
species such as Indo-Pacific hump-backed.

Where to look
Unlike the common bottlenose, the Indo-Pacific
bottlenose dolphin is found only in shallow coastal
waters – which makes it particularly vulnerable to
human disturbance and environmental degradation.
However, there is considerable overlap in the ranges
of the two species. The Indo-Pacific bottlenose lives
in tropical and sub-tropical regions of the western
Pacific and around the rim of the Indian Ocean as
far as the southern tip of Africa.

Commerson's Dolphin
Cephalorhynchus commersonii

ID FACT FILE

OTHER NAMES
Skunk dolphin, piebald dolphin, black and white dolphin.

MAXIMUM LENGTH
1.7 metres.

MAXIMUM WEIGHT
90 kilograms.

FIELD ID
Small, stocky body; black-and-white colouration (black-and-grey in Kerguelen); inconspicuous beak; conical head with gently-sloping forehead; rounded flippers; low-profile, broadly-rounded fin; black flippers, flukes and fin.

DIET
Mainly fish and crustaceans.

BREEDING
Calving interval unknown; gestation about 12 months.

A striking animal, with a stocky body and distinctive black-and-white markings, Commerson's dolphin is one of the smallest oceanic dolphins. It looks rather like a porpoise, but is very dolphin-like in its behaviour – a fast and active swimmer, it frequently rides the bow-waves of passing boats and is an enthusiastic breacher. It can often be seen swimming upside-down, spinning underwater as it goes, and seems to enjoy surfing in breakers close to shore. There is considerable variation in appearance from one individual to another, particularly in the extent of black and white. There is also a possible sub-species living around Kerguelen Island, in the Indian Ocean, which is significantly larger than its South American counterpart, has a better-defined beak and is black, white and grey rather than black and white.

Commerson's dolphin is named after a French scientist, Philibert Commerson, who sent the first description back to Europe after observing it in the Strait of Magellan in 1767.

Where to look

Commerson's dolphin is found in shallow coastal
waters, with the main centre of distribution in
cold temperate and sub-Antarctic waters around
southern Argentina, the extreme south of Chile in
Tierra del Fuego, and the Falkland Islands. There
is also an apparently isolated population around
Kerguelen Island in the Indian Ocean – more
than 8,000 kilometres away. Commerson's dolphins
were hunted for use as crab bait in Chile and
Argentina (now illegal) and are vulnerable to
drownings in gill nets.

Hector's Dolphin

Cephalorhynchus hectori

ID FACT FILE

OTHER NAMES
New Zealand
dolphin, little
pied dolphin.

MAXIMUM LENGTH
1.5 metres.

MAXIMUM WEIGHT
60 kilograms.

FIELD ID
Small, stocky
body; rounded
fin; conical head
with no beak;
complex colour
pattern (grey
forehead, light
grey upperside
and sides, white
underside with
finger-shaped
lobe pointing
towards tail);
broad black band
across eye to
flipper.

DIET
Fish and squid,
some
crustaceans.

BREEDING
Calves every 2–4
years; gestation
about 10–11
months.

Hector's dolphin is one of the smallest of all dolphins. A distinctive little animal, with a broad, black and rounded dorsal fin, it is found only in New Zealand. It can appear dark from a distance, but at close range has a striking, complex colour pattern of grey, black and white. It often bow-rides, especially in front of small, slow-moving boats, and is playful and acrobatic. Large numbers of Hector's dolphins are drowned in coastal gill nets, which may have reduced the population by more than half since the early 1970s. The Banks Peninsula Marine Mammal Sanctuary was established in 1989 to protect a key area of 1,170 square kilometres from commercial gill-netting and this has helped (but not entirely solved) the problem locally. In recent years, high-speed boats have been posing another serious threat. Hector's dolphin is now an endangered species: there could be as few as 100 individuals surviving around North Island and the population around South Island is numbered in low thousands.

Where to look
Found only in New Zealand, Hector's dolphin lives
in shallow coastal waters mainly off South Island
(there are two genetically distinct sub-populations:
one off the west coast and the other off the east and
south coasts). There is also a small remnant
population along the west coast of North Island. It
rarely ventures more than 10 kilometres offshore in
summer (usually just beyond the surf line or in
harbours), but at least some disperse further
offshore during winter.

Heaviside's Dolphin
Cephalorhynchus heavisidii

ID FACT FILE

OTHER NAMES
Benguela
dolphin, South
African dolphin.

MAXIMUM LENGTH
1.74 metres.

MAXIMUM WEIGHT
75 kilograms.

FIELD ID
Small, stocky
body; grey
anterior, dark
posterior; white
belly with lobes;
grey, cone-
shaped head;
indistinct beak;
dark patch
around eye;
prominent
triangular fin
about midway
along back; dark
flippers, fin and
flukes; small
groups of fewer
than 10 typical.

DIET
Variety of coastal
fish, squid and
octopus.

BREEDING
Possible calves
every 2–4 years;
gestation may be
10–11 months.

The enigmatic Heaviside's dolphin has long been shrouded in mystery. Our limited knowledge of this distinctive, porpoise-like dolphin is based mostly on opportunistic encounters rather than detailed studies. Even its name is rather confusing. It should have been named after Captain Haviside, who brought the first specimen from Africa to England in 1827, but was mistakenly named after Captain Heaviside, an eminent surgeon who collected anatomical specimens. However, in recent years there have been regular tours to see Heaviside's dolphins from Lambert's Bay, South Africa, and Walvis Bay, Namibia, offering a unique opportunity for some thrilling close encounters. True acrobats, the dolphins are thoroughly at home in turbulent water close to shore and can often be seen surfing or playing in the waves. They frequently leap high into the air, sometimes turning complete somersaults, and are keen bow-riders. Little is known about the status of Heaviside's dolphins, although unknown numbers are drowned in coastal fishing nets and there is evidence of limited hunting for their meat in some areas.

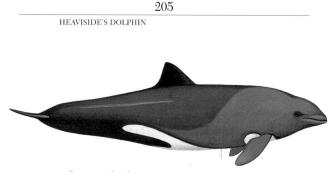

Where to look

Heaviside's dolphin has a very restricted range in shallow, coastal waters of South Africa and Namibia. It occurs from near the Angola-Namibia border (at about 17°S) south to Cape Point, South Africa (at about 34°S). It is normally within a few kilometres of shore in water less than 100 metres deep, but has been encountered 80 kilometres offshore in water 180 metres deep. It seems to be associated with the cold, northward-flowing Benguela Current.

Chilean Dolphin

Cephalorhynchus eutropia

ID FACT FILE

OTHER NAMES
White-bellied dolphin, black dolphin.

MAXIMUM LENGTH
1.7 metres.

MAXIMUM WEIGHT
65 kilograms.

FIELD ID
Small, stocky body; subtle dark pigmentation on upperside and sides, white underside (including throat); conical head with indistinct beak; pale grey forehead; white lips; large, rounded fin.

DIET
Fish, squid and crustaceans.

BREEDING
Possibly calves every 2–4 years; gestation about 10–11 months.

The Chilean dolphin tends to be quite a shy animal, particularly in the southern part of its range. One of the smallest of all cetaceans, it is known from a mixed collection of skeletons, a handful of strandings, and an increasing number of reliable sightings. It can appear all black at sea, but has a complex and rather subtle pigmentation of light and dark grey on the back and sides and a distinctive white belly and throat. However, the body colour darkens very quickly after death and this may account for its original name – the black dolphin – and for some of the inaccurate descriptions in early reports. The Chilean dolphin normally lives in small groups of two or three animals, although as many as 50 have been observed together and historical records report schools of several thousand. It is known to bow-ride in the north of its range, but hunting has made it wary in the south. It is hunted illegally for crab bait, and unknown numbers drown in coastal gill nets. The total population is probably numbered in low thousands.

Where to look

As its name suggests, the Chilean dolphin is found mainly in the cold, shallow, coastal waters of Chile. It lives along both open and sheltered coasts, from near Cape Horn (55°S) in the south to Valparaíso (about 33°S) in the north. It may sometimes occur at the extreme southern tip of Argentina, as well. It frequently enters small channels, estuaries and rivers, and seems to prefer areas with rapid tidal flow or turbulent water.

Hourglass Dolphin
Lagenorhynchus cruciger

ID FACT FILE

OTHER NAMES
Sea skunk.

MAXIMUM LENGTH
1.9 metres.

MAXIMUM WEIGHT
95 kilograms.

FIELD ID
Small, stocky body; sharply-demarcated black, white and grey markings; rough hourglass pattern on sides; short, black beak; large, falcate fin (variable in shape); black flippers, fin and flukes; fast swimmer.

DIET
Fish and squid, some crustaceans.

BREEDING
Calving interval and gestation period unknown.

Named for the crude black-and-white hourglass pattern on its sides, the hourglass dolphin is an inhabitant of remote Antarctic and sub-Antarctic seas. It has not been studied in detail and was originally named in 1824 from little more than rough drawings made at sea. Incredibly, no more than 20 specimens have been collected since. However, it is frequently encountered by cruise ships in the Drake Passage on their way to and from the Antarctic Peninsula, and seems to enjoy riding in their bow-waves and stern-waves. Its striking body markings – and the fact that it is the only dolphin with a dorsal fin consistently found in the open waters of the Southern Ocean – make it relatively easy to identify. Sometimes seen in association with fin whales, long-finned pilot whales, southern rightwhale dolphins and other cetaceans, and under large gatherings of feeding seabirds, hourglass dolphins usually live in small groups of about four to seven animals (although schools of more than 100 have

been recorded). Limited evidence suggests that
there may be a population of about 140,000 south of
the Antarctic Convergence.

Where to look
The hourglass dolphin is found in high latitudes of
the southern hemisphere, both north and south
of the Antarctic Convergence, mainly between
45°S and 60°S. It is predominantly oceanic, but
sometimes ventures right up to the ice-edge and
may be encountered relatively close to shore in
places like the South Shetland Islands. It has never
been systematically exploited.

Peale's Dolphin
Lagenorhynchus australis

ID FACT FILE

OTHER NAMES
Blackchin
dolphin.

MAXIMUM LENGTH
2.2 metres.

MAXIMUM WEIGHT
Possibly 115
kilograms.

FIELD ID
Robust body;
dark back with
single greyish-
white streak on
each side;
greyish-white
sides, white
underside;
predominantly
dark face and
chin; white
'armpits';
short, indistinct
beak; tall,
predominantly
greyish-black,
falcate fin.

DIET
Fish, squid,
octopuses and
crustaceans.

BREEDING
Calving interval
and gestation
period unknown.

Peale's dolphin resembles a dusky dolphin in overall appearance, but it has some distinctive features of its own: in particular, a dark face and brilliant white 'armpits'. Found only in southern South America and the Falkland Islands, it is sometimes described as an 'entrance dolphin' because it tends to be found in tide rips at the entrance to fjords and channels. Peale's dolphins are often observed swimming in shallow water parallel to shore, in small groups of about two to five animals (although as many as 100 have been seen together). They usually travel quite slowly, but will ride the bow-waves of large vessels or swim alongside smaller ones, and are perfectly capable of breaching and spyhopping. They often associate with Commerson's dolphins, which overlap in range. Peale's dolphins have been heavily exploited for use as bait in crab traps in southern Chile since at least the early 1970s and there has been a marked decrease in numbers in some areas. The scale of the hunting has declined, mainly because fishing effort is now directed more at sea urchins and less at crabs, but unknown numbers of dolphins are still being harpooned.

Where to look

Found in the coastal waters and over shallow
continental shelves of southern South America,
between about 38°S in the Pacific and 44°S in the
Atlantic, Peale's dolphins are often associated with
swift-flowing water. Particularly common around the
Falkland Islands and Tierra del Fuego, they often
greet returning Antarctic cruise ships as they
approach Cape Horn. They are frequently seen
close to shore near kelp beds.

Atlantic White-sided Dolphin

Lagenorhynchus acutus

ID FACT FILE

OTHER NAMES
Lag, white-side, jumper, springer.

MAXIMUM LENGTH
2.7 metres.

MAXIMUM WEIGHT
230 kilograms.

FIELD ID
Robust body with thick tail stock; black or dark grey upperside, grey stripe along flanks, white underside (extends onto side above flipper); white patch below fin and yellow or tan streak along each side of tail stock; short, thick beak; tall, falcate fin.

DIET
Fish and squid.

BREEDING
Calves every 2 years; gestation 11 months.

At first glance, the striking yellow or tan streak along each side of the Atlantic white-sided dolphin makes it look superficially similar to a common dolphin. But the position of the streak on the tail stock, and the complex and sharply demarcated pattern of bold grey, white and black on the rest of the body, make it quite a distinctive species at close

range. It is certainly one of the most colourful of all the world's dolphins. The Atlantic white-sided dolphin is a gregarious species, typically living in cohesive groups of between five and 50 (depending on the location) or looser aggregations of 500 or more. It often feeds in association with fin, humpback and other large whales, sometimes even riding their bow-waves, and will swim alongside slow ships and boats or bow-ride in front of faster ones.

Researchers often call it a 'lag', which is short for the scientific name *Lagenorhynchus*. A very rough population estimate of a few hundred thousand has been made for the entire North Atlantic.

Where to look

Atlantic white-sided dolphins are found in cold temperate and sub-Arctic waters of the northern North Atlantic, especially over the continental shelf and slope. Their range is remarkably similar to that of the white-beaked dolphin, with a band from northern Europe, through southern Greenland to Newfoundland, Nova Scotia and down the north-east coast of the States to Cape Cod. Several hundred get caught up and killed in the Faroese pilot whale hunt every year.

Pacific White-sided Dolphin

Lagenorhynchus obliquidens

ID FACT FILE

OTHER NAMES
Lag, Pacific
striped dolphin.

MAXIMUM LENGTH
2.5 metres.

MAXIMUM WEIGHT
180 kilograms.

FIELD ID
Robust body;
black or dark
grey upperside,
white underside;
large pale grey
patch above
flippers; bold
black line
demarcating
white belly; pale
grey streak on
sides; bicoloured
fin and flippers;
indistinct black-
tipped beak; tall,
broad-based,
falcate fin.

DIET
Fish and squid.

BREEDING
Possibly calves
every 2–3 years;
gestation about
12 months.

Pacific white-sided dolphins are great fun to watch. They often live in large schools containing hundreds or even thousands of individuals and are so lively and boisterous that their splashes can be seen long before it is possible to see the animals themselves. They leap into the air and spin or turn complete somersaults before splashing back into the water, and often ride the bow waves of passing boats or ships. Seen from above when they are bow-riding, the two narrow stripes down each side look like a pair of braces and are very distinctive. Pacific white-sided dolphins look remarkably similar to dusky dolphins and it has been suggested that the two belong to the same species; however, genetic evidence does not support this idea and there is no overlap in range. Like their Atlantic counterparts, they are gregarious animals and they can often be seen with other cetaceans, especially Risso's dolphins and northern rightwhale dolphins, as well as sea lions and seals. Researchers often call them 'lags', which is short for the scientific name *Lagenorhynchus*.

Where to look
Found in cold temperate waters across the northern
North Pacific, this fairly abundant species occurs
mainly offshore or in very deep water closer to
shore. Huge numbers were killed in high-seas drift
net fisheries, until this type of fishing was banned
in 1993, but hundreds still die in fishing nets set
within the 200 nautical mile limits of some
countries. The total population could be as high
as one million.

Dusky Dolphin
Lagenorhynchus obscurus

ID FACT FILE

Other names
None.

Maximum length
2.1 metres.

Maximum weight
90 kilograms.

Field ID
Small, robust body; predominantly dark upperside, white underside; two forward-pointing white or pale grey blazes along sides; prominent, falcate, two-toned fin; short, thick, dark beak; predominantly white face; small black patch around each eye.

Diet
Fish and squid.

Breeding
Calving interval unknown; gestation 11–13 months.

Dusky dolphins are social animals and seem to welcome the company of other species as well as their own. They frequently associate with a wide variety of whales and dolphins, as well as seals, a range of seabirds and even people. Very inquisitive animals, they frequently approach boats and sometimes play with people in the water. Well known for their high leaps and somersaults, 'duskies' are incredibly acrobatic; they often repeat their aerial displays dozens of times in a row and, when one animal starts, others may follow suit. Their group size varies from as few as 15 animals to as many as 500; larger gatherings tend to separate into small sub-groups to feed, but these join forces to socialise and rest. Duskies are remarkably similar to Pacific white-sided dolphins in appearance, although there is no overlap in range. In Peru, as many as 10,000 of them were killed every year during the mid-1980s; dolphin hunting has been banned there since 1993, but significant numbers are still being harpooned. Unknown but probably significant numbers drown in fishing nets throughout their range.

Where to look

Widely scattered in temperate waters throughout the southern hemisphere, the dusky dolphin is generally found in coastal and shelf waters. There are three main populations, in South America (including the Falkland Islands), south-western Africa and New Zealand (including Chatham, Auckland and Campbell Islands), as well as around several oceanic islands. It seems to be more abundant in the northern parts of its range in winter and in the southern parts in summer.

White-beaked Dolphin
Lagenorhynchus albirostris

ID FACT FILE

OTHER NAMES
Squidhound.

MAXIMUM LENGTH
3.1 metres.

MAXIMUM WEIGHT
350 kilograms.

FIELD ID
Very robust body;
predominantly
dark upperside,
white underside;
greyish-white
streak on each
side; pale area
on tail stock;
short, thick beak
(usually white,
but may be
brown or grey);
dark flippers, fin
and flukes; very
prominent fin.

DIET
Fish, squid,
octopuses and
crustaceans.

BREEDING
Calving interval
unknown;
gestation 10–11
months.

Despite its name, the white-beaked
dolphin does not always have a white
beak – it can be white, brown, light grey
or dark grey. Despite some exceptions
there is evidence to suggest that more
animals have white beaks in the east of
the range, and fewer in the west. The
two populations are morphologically
distinct and it is likely that they rarely
mix. The rather diffuse body pattern of
white, grey and black is also highly
variable between individuals. Strikingly
large and robust for a dolphin, the white-
beaked is capable of swimming at
considerable speed and is frequently
quite acrobatic. It can sometimes be
seen feeding with fin and humpback
whales, and with other dolphin species.
No detailed abundance estimates have
been made, but there are likely to be
many tens of thousands (if not hundreds
of thousands) across the North Atlantic.
It tends to be more common in Europe
than in North America.

Where to look
Found further north than any other
dolphin, the white-beaked dolphin is
widely distributed in cool temperate
and sub-Arctic waters of the northern
North Atlantic. Its distribution is broadly

similar to that of the Atlantic white-sided dolphin, although it occurs further into the Barents Sea and higher up both coasts of Greenland. Found mainly over the continental shelf, and also occasionally in shallow coastal waters.

Franciscana

Pontoporia blainvillei

ID FACT FILE

OTHER NAMES
La Plata dolphin.

MAXIMUM LENGTH
1.8 metres.

MAXIMUM WEIGHT
55 kilograms.

FIELD ID
Small body; grey
or brown
upperside and
sides, lighter
underside;
extremely long,
slender beak;
bulging melon;
broad, almost
triangular
flippers;
rounded, slightly
triangular fin set
behind midpoint
on back.

DIET
Mainly fish,
some squid,
octopuses and
crustaceans.

BREEDING
Calves every 2
years; gestation
10–11 months.

Despite its classification as a river
dolphin, the franciscana lives in the sea
and prefers shallow estuarine or coastal
waters. It is believed to feed mostly at or
near the seabed, probing for food and
even pulling away vegetation in its search
for suitable prey. An undemonstrative
and inconspicuous animal that seems to
spend much of its life alone, it is easy
to overlook in anything but the calmest
conditions. Consequently, it is poorly
known. It is one of the smallest of all
cetaceans and yet has the longest beak
(relative to body size) of any dolphin. The
beak of the juvenile is considerably
shorter than that of the adult, but its
relative length increases as the animal
grows older. There are no
distinctive colour markings
– franciscanas are

generally grey in the north of their range and slightly browner in the south. They are sometimes called La Plata dolphins, because the first specimen (described in 1844) was found in the Río de la Plata estuary, shared by Uruguay and Argentina. Significant numbers have been drowned in fishing nets since World War II and, living close to shore, they are particularly susceptible to habitat disturbance and pollution.

Where to look
Found in temperate coastal waters of eastern South America, the franciscana is known from Itaúnas in Espiritu Santo, Brazil, south to the northern coast of Golfo San Matías, in northern Patagonia, Argentina. Although it is common in the La Plata estuary, and some other estuaries, it does not travel upriver. It rarely ventures more than 60 kilometres offshore and is usually found in water that is less than 30 metres deep.

Yangtze River Dolphin

Lipotes vexillifer

ID FACT FILE

OTHER NAMES
Baiji, beiji, pei c'hi, whitefin dolphin, whiteflag dolphin, Chinese river dolphin.

MAXIMUM LENGTH
2.5 metres.

MAXIMUM WEIGHT
170 kilograms.

FIELD ID
Robust body; small head with rounded melon; bluish-grey upperside and sides, greyish-white or white underside; subtle, diffuse colour variations on face; long, narrow beak slightly upturned at tip; very low, triangular fin; tiny eyes; broad flippers.

DIET
Fish.

BREEDING
Calving interval unknown; gestation possibly 10–11 months.

The Yangtze river dolphin is the rarest and most endangered cetacean in the world. There were about 400 survivors in 1979–1980, 200 in 1986, fewer than 100 in 1989–1991, and no more than a couple of dozen in 1998. No-one knows exactly how many are left today, but there could be as few as 10 or 20 – or the species could already be extinct. An estimated 12 per cent of the entire human population lives in the basin of the dolphin's home in the Yangtze River, China, so it faces an inordinate number of threats. Dangerous fishing hooks, overfishing, heavy boat traffic, pollution, riverbank development and dam construction contrive to ensure that it is almost certainly doomed in its natural home. A single captive male called Qi-Qi (pronounced chee-chee)

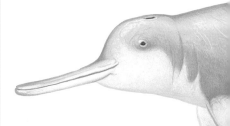

was a crucial source of information for many years.
He was rescued in 1980, after being injured by
fishing hooks, and remained in captivity until his
death, aged about 24, on 14 July 2002. Now the
future for the Yangtze river dolphin looks bleaker
than ever.

Where to look
Until recently, the Yangtze river dolphin was found
mainly in the middle and lower reaches of the
Yangtze River, in China (along a 1,700-kilometre
stretch from the mouth of the river). Its presence in
the Yangtze was recorded as long as 2,000 years ago.
Now absent from most or all of its former range, it
has always preferred areas where tributaries enter
the river, especially immediately upstream or
downstream of sandbanks or islets.

Indus River Dolphin

Platanista minor

ID FACT FILE

OTHER NAMES
Blind river
dolphin, bhulan.

MAXIMUM LENGTH
2.5 metres.

MAXIMUM WEIGHT
85 kilograms.

FIELD ID
Robust body;
uniform grey or
grey-brown colour
(sometimes with
pinkish
underside); long,
narrow beak
(thickens and
opens slightly
towards tip); low,
triangular hump
instead of fin;
small head with
rounded melon;
tiny eyes;
sneeze-like blow.

DIET
Fish and
crustaceans.

BREEDING
Calving interval
unknown;
gestation
possibly 12
months.

There has been considerable
uncertainty about the status of Indus
and Ganges river dolphins for many
years. Although living in different river
systems, and therefore separated
geographically, they look almost
identical and have remarkably similar
habits. First they were believed to be
the same species; then, in the 1970s,
differences in the structure of their
skulls and blood protein composition
were discovered, and it was decided
that they were two separate species. But
the study sample was very small and it
has all been thrown into doubt again, so
now many experts consider them to be
sub-species: *Platanista gangetica minor*
and *Platanista gangetica gangetica*. Like
its close relative, the Indus river dolphin
is normally found in very turbid, silt-

INDUS RIVER DOLPHIN

laden waters, and does not enter the sea. It is one of the most endangered cetaceans in the world and, until recently, was thought to be dangerously close to extinction. However, a recent survey estimated a total surviving population of at least 1,000 – not many, but considerably more than the low hundreds once feared.

Where to look
Found exclusively in the Indus River, in the Pakistani provinces of Sind and Punjab, the Indus river dolphin has been split into isolated pockets by dams and barrages built for irrigation and hydro-electric power generation. The majority of the population now lives at the downstream end of the range, between the Guddu and Sukkur barrages. They tend to congregate in the main channels during the dry season, dispersing into swollen creeks and minor tributaries during the monsoon.

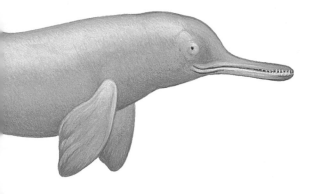

Ganges River Dolphin

Platanista gangetica

ID FACT FILE

OTHER NAMES
Ganges susu,
blind river
dolphin, Gangetic
dolphin.
MAXIMUM LENGTH
2.5 metres.
MAXIMUM WEIGHT
85 kilograms.
FIELD ID
Robust body;
uniform grey or
grey-brown colour
(sometimes with
pinkish
underside); long,
narrow beak
(thickens and
opens slightly
towards tip); low,
triangular hump
instead of fin;
small head with
rounded melon;
tiny eyes;
sneeze-like blow.
DIET
Fish and
crustaceans.
BREEDING
Calving interval
unknown;
gestation
possibly 12
months.

The Ganges and Indus river dolphins are the only cetaceans without a crystalline lens in their eyes. Their retinas do have light-gathering receptors, so they can probably detect the direction (and perhaps intensity) of light – but for all intents and purposes they are blind. Instead, they find their way around and catch food in their turbid riverine homes by building up a 'sound picture' of their surroundings, in much the same way that a bat navigates in the dark. They have an unusual swimming behaviour, which involves turning on one side, nodding the head and perhaps trailing a flipper in the mud to search for food. Both species can be difficult to find, but listen for their blows which, on calm days, can often be heard from quite far away; the Hindi name of the Ganges river dolphin, 'susu', is meant to imitate the sneeze-like sound made when they breathe. Both species face a great many threats, including entanglement in fishing gear, hunting, pollution, and dam and barrage construction. There is no reliable population estimate for the Ganges river dolphin, but it is probably in the low thousands.

Where to look

More widely distributed than its close relative in the Indus, the Ganges river dolphin is found in the Ganges, Meghna and Brahmaputra river systems of western India, Bangladesh, Nepal and Bhutan, and the Karnaphuli and Sangu rivers of Bangladesh. However, it is now virtually extinct in Nepal. Dams and barrages have fragmented the population throughout its range.

Amazon River Dolphin

Inia geoffrensis

ID FACT FILE

OTHER NAMES
Boto, pink
dolphin.

MAXIMUM LENGTH
2.5 metres.

MAXIMUM WEIGHT
180 kilograms.

FIELD ID
Long, rather
stocky body; vivid
pink, bluish-grey
or off-white
colour; low,
hump-like fin and
long ridge
towards tail; very
long beak;
bulbous melon
(shape can be
changed at will);
flexible neck;
large, triangular
flippers.

DIET
Mainly fish,
some
invertebrates
and small
turtles.

BREEDING
Calving interval
unknown;
gestation 10–11
months.

A strange-looking animal, with a pinkish body and enormous flippers, the Amazon river dolphin tends to be more playful than its closest relatives. It can be inquisitive and will sometimes approach boats or people in the water and has even been known to toss turtles into the air and grab fishermen's paddles. This is the largest of the river dolphins and, in the right areas, is the easiest to see. It often associates with the tucuxi, the only other cetacean in the Amazon Basin, and sometimes shares feeding grounds with giant otters. Its pinkish colour is caused by blood flow and becomes more accentuated when the animal is excited or aroused, but it is highly variable according to age, water clarity, temperature and location. There are

three recognised sub-species: in the Amazon River basin, the Madeira River Basin and the Orinoco River Basin. The Amazon river dolphin is the most abundant of the world's river dolphins, with an estimated population numbered in tens of thousands, but it is facing many threats common to all river dolphins, as well as deforestation in its rainforest home.

Where to look
Found in all the main rivers of the Amazon and Orinoco Basins (in Brazil, Colombia, Venezuela, Ecuador, Guyana, Peru and Bolivia), the Amazon river dolphin occurs more than 3,000 kilometres inland in some areas. In the dry season it is confined to the main rivers and tributaries, but in the rainy season it frequently enters flooded jungles and grasslands, swimming between the trees.

Vaquita
Phocoena sinus

ID FACT FILE

OTHER NAMES
Gulf of California
porpoise,
cochito.

MAXIMUM LENGTH
1.5 metres.

MAXIMUM WEIGHT
55 kilograms.

FIELD ID
Very small size;
stocky body
shape; complex
but subtle grey
cape, lighter grey
sides, white
underside;
prominent,
dolphin-like fin;
virtually no beak;
rounded head;
dark patch
around each eye;
dark stripe from
corner of beak to
flipper.

DIET
Fish and squid,
some
crustaceans.

BREEDING
Calves every
year; gestation
possibly 10–11
months.

One of the rarest and most endangered
marine cetaceans in the world, the
vaquita is very poorly known. Even on
official surveys around its home in the
northern Sea of Cortez, this very small
porpoise often eludes professional
biologists for days or even
weeks at a time.

It either avoids or ignores boats and
shows very little of itself at the surface.
Consequently, few people have ever seen
the species alive, and we know little
about its life and habits. At a recent
conference, one vaquita researcher made
a dismal prediction: 'probably in less than
10 years the vaquita will be extinct'.
Others are not quite so pessimistic, but
its future is undoubtedly bleak. There are
some 500–600 vaquitas left and an
estimated 39–84 are believed to drown in
gill nets every year – a huge number
considering the small size of the
surviving population. The Mexican
government established the Upper Gulf
of California and Colorado River Delta
Biosphere Reserve in 1993, but some 40

per cent of the vaquita population lives outside this protected area. More stringent conservation efforts are needed urgently if it is to survive.

Where to look
The vaquita probably has the most restricted distribution of any marine cetacean. It survives only in the extreme northern end of the Sea of Cortez (Gulf of California) in western Mexico (north of 30°45'N). Most common around the Colorado River Delta, it is usually seen within 11–25 kilometres of shore and is rarely encountered in water much deeper than 40 metres (usually 11–50 metres).

Harbour Porpoise
Phocoena phocoena

ID FACT FILE

OTHER NAMES
Common
porpoise, puffing
pig, puffer.
MAXIMUM LENGTH
1.9 metres.
MAXIMUM WEIGHT
80 kilograms.
FIELD ID
Small size;
robust body;
nondescript
colouring (grey
upperside, lighter
sides and
underside);
triangular fin
(large relative to
visible portion of
back when
surfacing);
indistinct beak;
small, conical
head; one or
more dark
stripes from
mouth to flipper.
DIET
Mainly fish,
some squid and
octopuses;
crustaceans
(calves only).
BREEDING
Calves every 1–2
years; gestation
10–11 months.

The harbour porpoise is the most widespread and commonly seen of all the porpoises. However, it is generally wary of boats and rarely bow-rides. A brief glimpse of its dark back and low, triangular dorsal fin is all this undemonstrative little cetacean usually shows of itself. When it rises to breathe, the lasting impression is of a slow, forward-rolling motion, as if the dorsal fin is mounted on a revolving wheel lifted briefly above the surface and then withdrawn. As with most dolphins and porpoises, its blow is rarely seen – but it can sometimes be heard and sounds rather like a sneeze, giving the harbour porpoise one of its alternative names, the puffing pig. Like all porpoises, it has spade-shaped teeth – quite unlike the conical teeth of dolphins. Once hunted intensively in Europe for its meat and blubber (especially in the seventeenth and eighteenth centuries), it is now protected in most of its range. However, the biggest threat to harbour porpoises today is incidental capture in gill nets, herring weirs and other fishing equipment, which drown many thousands every year.

Where to look

Found in cool temperate and sub-Arctic waters
of the northern hemisphere, the harbour
porpoise is usually seen within 10 kilometres of land.
It frequents relatively shallow bays, estuaries and
tidal channels less than about 200 metres in depth.
There are three distinct populations, which are
reproductively isolated and classified as separate
sub-species: in the North Atlantic, the North Pacific
and the Black Sea.

Burmeister's Porpoise

Phocoena spinipinnis

ID FACT FILE

OTHER NAMES
Black porpoise.

MAXIMUM LENGTH
1.9 metres.

MAXIMUM WEIGHT
105 kilograms.

FIELD ID
Small, stocky body; predominantly dark grey or black, lighter underside; backward-leaning fin (further back than on any other small cetacean); conical head; flattened forehead; indistinct beak; dark eye patch; dark grey stripe from chin to flipper.

DIET
Mainly fish, some squid and crustaceans.

BREEDING
Probably calves every 1–2 years; gestation 11–12 months.

Easily recognised by its small size and backward-pointing dorsal fin, Burmeister's porpoise is nevertheless rather inconspicuous and rarely seen. It will often accelerate and swim away when approached by a boat. However, it is believed to be considerably more abundant than the limited number of sightings would otherwise suggest, especially in the Strait of Magellan and Beagle Channel, around Tierra del Fuego. The dorsal fin is unique among cetaceans – it really does look as if it is leaning backwards, pointing towards the tail, and has a series of small tubercles (knob-like prominences) on the leading edge that become sharper as the animal grows older. Typically seen alone or in pairs (with occasional temporary aggregations of eight or more), Burmeister's porpoises normally appear completely dark at sea. Hundreds or even thousands of them are hunted for

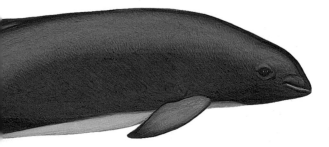

human food and bait every year, especially in Peru and Chile, and they are believed to be caught and drowned in a variety of fishing nets throughout much of their range.

Where to look
Burmeister's porpoise is found in the shallow coastal waters of South America. Its range extends from Cape Horn north as far as Bahía de Paita, in northern Peru, on the Pacific side and as far as Santa Catarine, in southern Brazil, on the Atlantic side. Limited evidence suggests that it is most common close to shore in summer (sometimes inside the kelp line and even in the lower reaches of rivers) and up to 50 kilometres offshore in winter.

Finless Porpoise

Neophocaena phocaenoides

ID FACT FILE

OTHER NAMES
Black porpoise, black finless porpoise, jiangzhu.

MAXIMUM LENGTH
2 metres.

MAXIMUM WEIGHT
90 kilograms.

FIELD ID
Very small size; slender body; pale blue-grey or grey body colour, slightly paler underside; dorsal ridge but no fin; small head and no beak; rounded melon; long, pointed flippers; good head mobility.

DIET
Fish, squid, octopuses, cuttlefish and crustaceans.

BREEDING
Probably calves every 2 years; gestation about 11 months.

One of the smallest of all cetaceans, the finless porpoise is the only porpoise without a dorsal fin and, consequently, looks rather like a small beluga. Instead of a fin it has a long ridge with a line of circular bumps, known as tubercles, which may be used by the female as an anti-slip device to 'carry' its calf. Despite two of its alternative names, it is normally a pale blue-grey colour (although some populations darken with age and they often turn black after death). It is the only porpoise in the region, apart from a slight overlap in range with harbour porpoises in Japan and the Sea of Japan. Finless porpoises are usually difficult to observe, rarely leaping from the water and never bow-riding, but some populations are more approachable: there are even commercial trips to see them in northern Kyushu, Japan. The species has virtually disappeared from much of its former range, mainly because of incidental capture in fishing nets. It also suffers for living close to shore – from pollution, overfishing, deforestation of mangrove swamps and disturbance.

Where to look

Finless porpoises are found in warm, coastal waters and some major river systems in the Indo-Pacific. Their range stretches from the Persian Gulf to

northern Japan and down to Java (and, possibly, to New Guinea and northern Australia). They are rarely more than a few kilometres from land and occur in both saltwater and freshwater. One of the best-known populations lives in the Yangtze River, China, where they are found up to 1,600 kilometres from the sea.

Spectacled Porpoise
Phocoena dioptrica

ID FACT FILE

OTHER NAMES
None.

MAXIMUM LENGTH
2.2 metres.

MAXIMUM WEIGHT
115 kilograms.

FIELD ID
Small, robust body; jet black upperside, white underside; male has high rounded fin, female has lower, more triangular fin; small, rounded head with no beak; black eye patch with white 'spectacles'; black lips.

DIET
Fish and crustaceans, possibly squid.

BREEDING
Calving interval and gestation period unknown.

Named for the fine white line around each eye, the spectacled porpoise is rarely seen even in its apparent stronghold along the wild, Atlantic beaches of Tierra del Fuego, at the extreme southern tip of South America. Until 1976, the species was known from only nine specimens and one sighting and even today most information comes from weathered bones and carcasses washed ashore. The striking, clearly demarcated jet-black and white markings are distinctive. Interestingly, the two sexes are quite different in appearance: the male has a large, rounded dorsal fin, while the female's is much smaller and more triangular in shape. There has long been confusion over its taxonomy – it was originally placed in the genus *Phocoena* with most of the other porpoises, then in the mid-1980s was placed in a separate genus, *Australophocaena*, but recently it was returned to *Phocoena*. Remains of spectacled porpoises have been found in

6,000-year-old kitchen middens of the canoe people in Tierra del Fuego. Little is known about the threats they face today, but they certainly drown in gill nets and trawls.

Where to look
Known mostly from cold temperate and sub-Antarctic waters around the southern Atlantic coast of South America and New Zealand and Australia, the spectacled porpoise is found in both coastal and offshore waters. Its distribution appears to be circumpolar because there are records from widely separate islands across the southern hemisphere, including the Falklands, South Georgia, Kerguelen, Heard, Macquarie and Auckland.

Dall's Porpoise
Phocoenoides dalli

ID FACT FILE

OTHER NAMES
Spray porpoise,
white-flanked
porpoise, True's
porpoise.
MAXIMUM LENGTH
2.4 metres.
MAXIMUM WEIGHT
200 kilograms.
FIELD ID
Small size;
exceptionally
stocky body;
sharply
demarcated
black-and-white
markings;
prominent,
triangular fin
(slightly falcate
at tip); white
patch on
otherwise black
fin and flukes;
tiny head in
relation to body;
indistinct beak;
distinctive spray
when surfacing.
DIET
Fish and squid.
BREEDING
Calves every
year; gestation
10–12 months.

Dall's porpoise is the fastest of the small cetaceans and is usually seen as a blur when it breaks the surface at high speed. It produces a distinctive spray of water called the 'rooster tail', which is made by a cone of water coming off the head as it rises to breathe and can almost obscure the animal itself. It is a very distinctive porpoise, with an exceptionally stocky body and striking markings: mostly black but with brilliant white patches on the sides and underside. There are two distinct forms: the Dalli-type, which occurs throughout the range and has a smaller area of white on the flanks; and the Truei-type, which is found only in the western North Pacific and has more white. Unlike most other porpoises, it often approaches boats and readily bow-rides (although it soon loses interest in vessels travelling too slowly). Huge numbers are killed by drift-net fisheries and large numbers die in a variety of other fishing equipment. Nearly 20,000 are killed every year in Japan to provide meat for human consumption. The total population is probably in the order of several hundred thousand.

DALL'S PORPOISE

Where to look

Dall's porpoises live in the cool temperate waters of the North Pacific, and adjacent seas (Bering Sea, Okhotsk Sea and Sea of Japan). They are mainly oceanic but are found close to shore where the water is sufficiently deep, such as over deep-water canyons. There may be a seasonal shift in some areas: north and offshore in summer, south and inshore in winter.

SPECIES CHECKLIST

Baleen Whales

Family: Balaenidae

1. North Atlantic right whale (*Eubalaena glacialis*)
2. North Pacific right whale (*Eubalaena japonica*)
3. Southern right whale (*Eubalaena australis*)
4. Bowhead whale (*Balaena mysticetus*)

Family: Neobalaenidae

5. Pygmy right whale (*Caperea marginata*)

Family: Eschrichtiidae

6. Grey whale (*Eschrichtius robustus*)

Family: Balaenopteridae

7. Humpback whale (*Megaptera novaeangliae*)
8. Minke whale (*Balaenoptera acutorostrata*)
9. Antarctic minke whale (*Balaenoptera bonaerensis*)
10. Bryde's whale (*Balaenoptera edeni*)
11. Sei whale (*Balaenoptera borealis*)
12. Fin whale (*Balaenoptera physalus*)
13. Blue whale (*Balaenoptera musculus*)

Toothed Whales

Family: Physeteridae

14.   Sperm whale *(Physeter macrocephalus)*

Family: Kogiidae

15.   Pygmy sperm whale *(Kogia breviceps)*
16.   Dwarf sperm whale *(Kogia sima)*

Family: Monodontidae

17.   Narwhal *(Monodon monoceros)*
18.   Beluga *(Delphinapterus leucas)*

Family: Ziphiidae

19.   Arnoux's beaked whale *(Berardius arnuxii)*
20.   Baird's beaked whale *(Berardius bairdii)*
21.   Longman's beaked whale *(Indopacetus pacificus)*
22.   Shepherd's beaked whale *(Tasmacetus shepherdi)*
23.   Cuvier's beaked whale *(Ziphius cavirostris)*
24.   Northern bottlenose whale *(Hyperoodon ampullatus)*
25.   Southern bottlenose whale *(Hyperoodon planifrons)*
26.   Pygmy beaked whale *(Mesoplodon peruvianus)*
27.   Bahamonde's beaked whale *(Mesoplodon traversii)*
28.   Sowerby's beaked whale *(Mesoplodon bidens)*
29.   Andrews' beaked whale *(Mesoplodon bowdoini)*
30.   Hubbs' beaked whale *(Mesoplodon carlhubbsi)*
31.   Blainville's beaked whale *(Mesoplodon densirostris)*
32.   Gervais' beaked whale *(Mesoplodon europaeus)*
33.   Ginkgo-toothed beaked whale *(Mesoplodon ginkgodens)*

34. Gray's beaked whale (*Mesoplodon grayi*)
35. Hector's beaked whale (*Mesoplodon hectori*)
36. Strap-toothed whale (*Mesoplodon layardii*)
37. True's beaked whale (*Mesoplodon mirus*)
38. Stejneger's beaked whale (*Mesoplodon stejnegeri*)
39. Perrin's beaked whale (*Mesoplodon perrini*)

Family: Delphinidae

40. Pygmy killer whale (*Feresa attenuata*)
41. False killer whale (*Pseudorca crassidens*)
42. Melon-headed whale (*Peponocephala electra*)
43. Long-finned pilot whale (*Globicephala melas*)
44. Short-finned pilot whale (*Globicephala macrorhynchus*)
45. Killer whale (*Orcinus orca*)

46. Risso's dolphin (*Grampus griseus*)
47. Irrawaddy dolphin (*Orcaella brevirostris*)
48. Tucuxi (*Sotalia fluviatilis*)
49. Spinner dolphin (*Stenella longirostris*)
50. Clymene dolphin (*Stenella clymene*)
51. Striped dolphin (*Stenella coeruleoalba*)
52. Pantropical spotted dolphin (*Stenella attenuata*)
53. Atlantic spotted dolphin (*Stenella frontalis*)
54. Atlantic hump-backed dolphin (*Sousa teuszii*)
55. Indo-Pacific hump-backed dolphin (*Sousa chinensis*)
56. Northern rightwhale dolphin (*Lissodelphis borealis*)
57. Southern rightwhale dolphin (*Lissodelphis peronii*)
58. Long-beaked common dolphin (*Delphinus capensis*)
59. Short-beaked common dolphin (*Delphinus delphis*)
60. Rough-toothed dolphin (*Steno bredanensis*)
61. Fraser's dolphin (*Lagenodelphis hosei*)
62. Common bottlenose dolphin (*Tursiops truncatus*)
63. Indo-Pacific bottlenose dolphin (*Tursiops aduncus*)
64. Commerson's dolphin (*Cephalorhynchus commersonii*)
65. Hector's dolphin (*Cephalorhynchus hectori*)

66.   Heaviside's dolphin *(Cephalorhynchus heavisidii)*
67.   Chilean dolphin *(Cephalorhynchus eutropia)*
68.   Hourglass dolphin *(Lagenorhynchus cruciger)*
69.   Peale's dolphin *(Lagenorhynchus australis)*
70.   Dusky dolphin *(Lagenorhynchus obscurus)*
71.   Atlantic white-sided dolphin *(Lagenorhynchus acutus)*
72.   Pacific white-sided dolphin *(Lagenorhynchus obliquidens)*
73.   White-beaked dolphin *(Lagenorhynchus albirostris)*

Family: Iniidae

74.   Amazon river dolphin *(Inia geoffrensis)*

Family: Lipotidae

75.   Yangtze river dolphin *(Lipotes vexillifer)*

Family: Pontoporiidae

76.   Franciscana *(Pontoporia blainvillei)*

Family: Platanistidae

77.   Indus river dolphin *(Platanista minor)*
78.   Ganges river dolphin *(Platanista gangetica)*

Family: Phocoenidae

79.   Vaquita *(Phocoena sinus)*
80.   Harbour porpoise *(Phocoena phocoena)*
81.   Burmeister's porpoise *(Phocoena spinipinnis)*
82.   Spectacled porpoise *(Phocoena dioptrica)*
83.   Finless porpoise *(Neophocaena phocaenoides)*
84.   Dall's porpoise *(Phocoenoides dalli)*

GLOSSARY

Amphipod – small, shrimp-like crustacean that is a food source for some whales.

Baleen/baleen plates – comb-like plates hanging down from the upper jaws of most large whales; used instead of teeth to capture prey.

Baleen whale – sub-order of whales with baleen plates instead of teeth, known in the scientific world as Mysticeti.

Beak – elongated snout of many cetaceans.

Blow – cloud of water vapour exhaled by cetaceans (also known as the spout); often used to describe the act of breathing.

Blowhole(s) – nasal opening(s) or nostril(s) on the top of the head.

Blubber – layer of fat just beneath the skin of marine mammals; important for insulation instead of fur.

Bow-riding – riding in the pressure wave in front of a boat, ship or big whale.

Breaching – leaping completely (or almost completely) out of the water, and landing back with a splash.

Bubble-netting – feeding technique used by humpback whales in which they produce fishing nets by blowing bubbles underwater.

Callosity – area of roughened skin on the head of a right whale, to which whale lice and barnacles attach.

Cetacean – any member of the order Cetacea, which includes all whales, dolphins and porpoises.

Copepod – a small crustacean that is a food source for some whales.

Crustacean – member of a class of invertebrates (animals without backbones) that is a food source for many marine animals; mostly aquatic.

Dorsal fin – raised structure on the back of most (but not all) cetaceans; not supported by bone.

Drift net – fishing net which hangs in the water, unseen and undetectable, and is carried freely with the ocean currents and winds; strongly criticised for catching everything in its path, from seabirds and turtles to whales and dolphins.

Echolocation – process of sending out sounds and interpreting the returning echoes to build up a sound picture, as in sonar; used by many cetaceans to orientate, navigate and find food.

Flipper – flattened, paddle-shaped limb of a marine mammal; refers to the front limb of a cetacean (also known as the pectoral fin).

Flipper-slapping – raising a flipper out of the water and slapping it onto the surface.

Fluke – horizontally flattened tail of a cetacean; contains no bone.

Fluking – raising the tail flukes into the air upon diving.

Gill net – similar to a drift net in design, although much smaller and fixed in one position near the coast or in a river.

Hydrophone – waterproofed, underwater microphone.

Keel – distinctive bulge on the tail stock near the flukes.

Krill – small, shrimp-like crustaceans that form the major food of many large whales; there are about 80 different species, ranging from 8-60mm in length.

Lobtailing – slapping tail flukes against the water, creating a splash.

Logging – lying still at or near the surface.

Mandible – lower jaw of the skull.

Melon – fatty organ in the bulging forehead of many toothed cetaceans, believed to be used to focus sounds for echolocation.

Pectoral fin – see flipper.

Photo-identification – technique for studying cetaceans using photographs as a permanent record of identifiable individuals.

Pod – co-ordinated group of whales; normally used for larger, toothed whales.

Polar – region around either the North Pole or South Pole (i.e. Arctic or Antarctic).

Porpoising – leaping out of the water while swimming at speed.

Purse-seine net – long net set around a shoal of fish, then gathered at the bottom and drawn in to form a purse.

Rorqual – baleen whale of the genus *Balaenoptera*; many experts also include the humpback whale (genus *Megaptera*) in this group.

Rostrum – upper jaw of the skull (may be used to refer to the beak or snout).

School – co-ordinated group of cetaceans; term normally used in association with dolphins.

Snout – see beak.

Sonar – see echolocation.

Spout – see blow.

Spyhopping – raising the head vertically out of the water, apparently to look around above the surface.

Submarine canyon – deep, steep-sided valley in the continental shelf.

Tail stock – muscular region of the tail between the flukes and the dorsal fin.

Temperate – mid-latitude regions between the tropics and the poles.

Toothed whale – sub-order of whales with teeth, known in the scientific world as Odontoceti.

Tropical – low-latitude regions of the world between the tropics of Capricorn and Cancer.

Tubercle – circular bumps found on some cetaceans; usually along the edges of flippers and dorsal fins, but also on a humpback whale's head.

Turbid – muddy or cloudy water carrying lots of sediment.

Wake-riding – swimming in the frothy wake of a boat or ship.

Whalebone – another name for baleen.

FURTHER READING

There are far too many excellent books on whales, dolphins and
porpoises to list them all. But here is a small and varied selection:

Carwardine, Mark, Hoyt, Erich, Fordyce, R. Ewan and Gill, Peter,
Whales & Dolphins: The Ultimate Guide to Marine Mammals,
HarperCollins, 1998.

Darling, James D., Nicklin, Charles Flip, Norris, Kenneth S.,
Whitehead, Hal and Warsig, Bernd, *Whales, Dolphins and
Porpoises*, National Geographic Society, Washington, 1995.

Ford, John K.B., Ellis, Graeme M. and Balcomb, Kenneth C.,
Killer Whales, UBC Press, 2000.

Hoyt, Erich, *Marine Protected Areas For Whales Dolphins and
Porpoises*, Earthscan, 2005.

Katona, Steven and Lien, Jon, *A Guide to the Photographic
Identification of Individual Whales*, American Cetacean
Society, 1990.

Leatherwood, Stephen and Reeves, Randall R., *The Sierra Club
Handbook of Whales and Dolphins*, Sierra Club Books, 1983.

Mann, J., Connor, R.C., Tyack, P.L. and Whitehead, H. (eds),
Cetacean Societies: Field Studies of Dolphins and Whales,
University of Chicago Press, 2000.

Payne, Stefani, *Arctic Whales*, Greystone Books, 1995.

Perrin, William F., Wursig, Bernd and Thewissen, J.G.M. (eds),
Encyclopedia of Marine Mammals, Academic Press, 2002.

Reeves, Randall R., Stewart, Brent S., Clapham, Phillip J., Powell, James A. and Folkens, Pieter, A., *Sea Mammals of the World*, A&C Black, 2002.

Reeves, R.R., Smith, B.D., Crespo, E.A., Notarbartolo di Sciara, G., *Dolphins, Whales and Porpoises: 2002–2010 Conservation Action Plan for the World's Cetaceans*, IUCN, 2002.

Simmonds, Mark P. and Hutchinson, Judith D. (eds), *The Conservation of Whales and Dolphins: Science and Practice*, J. Wiley, 1996.

Simmonds, Mark, *Whales and Dolphins of the World*, New Holland, 2004.

Waller, Geoffrey (ed), *Sealife: A Complete Guide to the Marine Environment*, Pica Press, 1996.

Whitehead, H., *Sperm Whales: Social Evolution in the Ocean*, University of Chicago Press, 2003.

WorldLife Library (various authors), *Blue Whales; Minke Whales; Humpback Whales; Grey Whales; Sperm Whales; Right Whales; Killer Whales; Beluga Whales; Bottlenose Dolphins; Porpoises*; Colin Baxter, 1994–2004.

INDEX

 **Collins**

If you have enjoyed this book, why not have a look at
some of the other titles in the WILD GUIDE series?

Garden Birds	0 00 717789 5
Birds	0 00 717792 5
Wild Flowers	0 00 717793 3
Insects	0 00 717795 X
Night Sky	0 00 717790 9
Night Sky Starfinder	0 00 717791 7
Weather	0 00 716072 0
Seashore	0 00 716071 2
Trees	0 00 719152 9
Butterflies	0 00 719131 0
Mushrooms	0 00 719150 2
Rocks and Minerals	0 00 717794 1
British Wildlife	0 00 719172 3

Other titles of interest from Collins:

Field Guide Sharks	0 00 713610 2
Gem Sharks	0 00 721986 5
Pocket Guide Fish	0 00 219945 9
Gem Fish	0 00 718013 6

To order any of these titles please call **08707871724**.

www.collins.co.uk